RETRIEV,

IN CATHOLIC THOUGHT

The middle years of this century marked a particularly intense time of crisis and change in European society. During this period (1930-1950), a broad intellectual and spiritual movement arose within the European Catholic community, largely in response to the secularism that lay at the core of the crisis. The movement drew inspiration from earlier theologians and philosophers such as Möhler, Newman, Gardeil, Rousselot, and Blondel, as well as from men of letters like Charles Péguy and Paul Claudel.

The group of academic theologians included in the movement extended into Belgium and Germany, in the work of men like Emile Mersch, Dom Odo Casel, Romano Guardini, and Karl Adam. But above all the theological activity during this period centered in France. Led principally by the Jesuits at Fourviére and the Dominicans at Le Saulchoir, the French revival included many of the greatest names in twentieth-century Catholic thought: Henri de Lubac, Jean Daniélou, Yves Congar, Marie-Dominique Chenu, Louis Bouyer, and, in association, Hans Urs von Balthasar.

It is not true — as subsequent folklore has it — that those theologians represented any sort of self-conscious "school": indeed, the differences among them were important. At the same time, they were united in the double conviction that theology had to speak to the present situation, and that the condition for doing so faithfully lay in a recovery of the Church's past. In other words, they all saw clearly that the first step in what later came to be known as *aggiornamento* had to be *ressourcement* — a rediscovery of the riches of the whole of the Church's two thousand year tradition. According to de Lubac, for example, all of his own works as well as the entire *Sources chrétiennes* collection are based on the presupposition that "the renewal of Christian vitality is linked at least partially to a renewed exploration of the periods and of the works where the Christian tradition is expressed with particular intensity."

In sum, for the *ressourcement* theologians theology involved a "return to the sources" of Christian faith, for the purpose of drawing out the meaning and significance of these sources for the critical questions of our time. What these theologians sought was a spiritual and intellectual communion with Christianity in its most vital moments as transmitted to us in its classic texts, a communion which would nourish, invigorate, and rejuvenate twentieth-century Catholicism.

The *ressourcement* movement bore great fruit in the documents of the Second Vatican Council and has deeply influenced the work of Pope John Paul II and Cardinal Joseph Ratzinger, Prefect of the Sacred Congregation of the Doctrine of the Faith.

The present series is rooted in this twentieth-century renewal of theology, above all as the renewal is carried in the spirit of de Lubac and von Balthasar. In keeping with that spirit, the series understands *ressourcement* as revitalization: a return to the sources, for the purpose of developing a theology that will truly meet the challenges of our time. Some of the features of the series, then, will be:

- a return to classical (patristic-mediaeval) sources;

- a renewed interpretation of St. Thomas;

- a dialogue with the major movements and thinkers of the twentieth century, with particular attention to problems associated with the Enlightenment, modernity, liberalism.

The series will publish out-of-print or as yet untranslated studies by earlier authors associated with the *ressourcement* movement. The series also plans to publish works by contemporary authors sharing in the aim and spirit of this earlier movement. This will include interpretations of de Lubac and von Balthasar and, more generally, any works in theology, philosophy, history, and literature which give renewed expression to a classic Catholic sensibility.

The editor of the Ressourcement series, David L. Schindler, is Gagnon Professor of Fundamental Theology at the John Paul II Institute in Washington, D.C., and editor of the North American edition of *Communio: International Catholic Review,* a federation of journals in thirteen countries founded in Europe in 1972 by Hans Urs von Balthasar, Jean Daniélou, Henri de Lubac, Joseph Ratzinger, and others.

Letters from Lake Como

Explorations in Technology and the Human Race

Romano Guardini

With an Introduction by
Louis Dupré

Translated by
Geoffrey W. Bromiley

WILLIAM B. EERDMANS PUBLISHING COMPANY
GRAND RAPIDS, MICHIGAN / CAMBRIDGE, U.K.

First published in German as *Die Technik und der Mensch: Briefe vom Comer See*
© 1981, 1990 (second edition) by Matthias-Grünewald-Verlag, Mainz.

First English edition © 1994 Wm. B. Eerdmans Publishing Co.

Published 1994 by
Wm. B. Eerdmans Publishing Co.
2140 Oak Industrial Drive N.E., Grand Rapids, Michigan 49505 /
P.O. Box 163 Cambridge CB3 9PU U.K.

Printed in the United States of America

00 99 98 97 96 95 94   7 6 5 4 3 2 1

Library of Congress Cataloging-in-Publication Data

Guardini, Romano, 1885-1968.
[Briefe vom Comer See. English]
Letters from Lake Como: explorations in technology and the human race /
Romano Guardini; with an introduction by Louis Dupré;
translated by Geoffrey W. Bromiley.
p.   cm.
ISBN 978-0-8028-0108-1
1. Technology and civilization.
I. Bromiley, Geoffrey William.   II. Title.
CB478.G813   1994
303.48'3 — dc20   93-39533
                                       CIP

www.eerdmans.com

Contents

Preface

These letters initially appeared in the *Schildgenossen*, the first in the Pentecost copy in 1923 and the last in the fall copy of 1925. In answer to requests I am now publishing them in this separate edition. In all essentials they have retained their original form, even though many arguments might be advanced against this. A path leads from the first letter to the last, on which many things became clearer to the author and were expanded and changed. It would have been natural to revise the whole series in the light of the insights gained. But the letters were not concerned simply with the philosophy of culture. It thus seemed permissible and right to let them stand as they are, i.e., as testimonies to the path taken with all that proved to be unattainable and even wrong on it. Perhaps they will be welcome as such to others also on the road "between the times."

To say that, however, is also to say that the road continues. Hence the ninth letter, whether in its thoughts or in its attitude, must not be regarded as definitive. It is indeed particularly incomplete and hardly does justice to its theme. Today already I would say much in it differently, yet not in the sense of deviating from the inner line and above all not in the sense of retracting. That is what justifies me in again presenting the letters to my readers, even though they come from hours that are long since past.

Varenna on Lake Como,
September 1926

Preface to the Fifth Edition

Since the letters from Lake Como were first published almost thirty-five years have gone by. During this period the development of which these letters speak has moved ahead with great power. It has become so familiar to all of us that to many a reader the letters might seem to be "romantic." In the meantime I myself have learned to see things more profoundly. I would thus ask my readers to see in this book the expression of a first encounter with problems its author took up again more thoroughly in later works, especially *Das Ende der Neuzeit,* Würzburg 1959, and *Die Macht,* Würzburg 1959,[1] and *Kultur als Werk und Gefährdung* and *Der unvollständige Mensch und die Macht,* both Würzburg.[2]

Munich 1960

1. These two works were brought out in a new edition, Mainz 1989.
2. These works are now available in *Sorge um den Menschen,* vol. 1 of *Werke,* Mainz 1988.

Introduction

This short book may well be the jewel in the crown of Guardini's writings. Its casual format of occasional letters has preserved the freshness of the author's original vision. Returning to the homeland he never knew — Guardini's parents emigrated to Germany when he was one year old — he records impressions as they reach him, feelingly but without preestablished order. As the wandering continues, observations turn into symbols. Ideas long held and theoretically articulated here assume the concrete shape of visual intuition and nostalgic emotion. If Guardini's theoretical works contain the justification, the *Letters* present the vision. One may disagree with his concept of modern culture — wishing to rearrange the chain of cause and effect, or at least to replace the accents — but it is difficult not to share his vision. In the *Letters* "ideas" return to what they were originally: not abstract universals but contemplated forms. Around the ancient lake the visitor witnesses the delayed victory of the modern world over the remains of classical culture and the traditional Christian one that assumed it.

When in 1900 Guardini published his *Letters* they required no introduction. Their author stood at the center of religious and intellectual life in Germany. Educated Christians had read his studies on Socrates, Pascal, Dostoyevsky, Hölderin, Rilke, as well as his probing search of what characterizes the Christian worldview. He was an unusually reticent and intensely private man, yet his eloquence drew thousands of listeners to his lectures at the universities of Tübingen and München. It was the obliqueness, the unfinished allusiveness of his thought as much as the power of his thinking and the elegance of its expression that attracted an audience profoundly shaken by the war in its previously held certainties. Guardini did not "preach," even though he was a priest; nor did he "theologize," even though he occupied a chair of theology. Listening to the great voices of his age, he mused on the human condition in the light of faith. "Living faith means dynamic life," he wrote in *Faith and Modern Man*. His style reflects the restlessness of the modern mind, constantly shifting its perspectives, endlessly questioning its conclusions. Yet underneath the moving thought, the reader feels the stable peace of a mind secure in a timeless faith.

When Guardini's work first appeared, our country was not ready for a knowledgeable reception. Today his light has waned, even in Europe. Recent thought, especially religious thought, has moved so fast in so many unexpected ways that the present generation hardly recognizes the language of the previous one. A cultural ride at top speed has left us breathless with no time for reflection. In a period of frantic change, no thinkers vanish more rapidly than those of the recent past. Their ideas are not so much refuted as shoved aside for a succession of new ones that address the present more directly. We secretly fear the ideas of the past — not those of the remote past but of the past still remembered. Their growing paleness reminds us uncomfortably of the transiency of our own thought. For those who succeed in overcoming the aversion to the "imperfect past," however, the time has arrived to revisit a thinker whom we failed to understand when he was still with us. *Letters from Lake Como* provides the most attractive and least constrictive entrance to Guardini's multifaceted thought. Its pages, conceived while the author was sailing from one shore to the other or walking from one village to the next, summon us to reconsider our position in the realm of being.

In the *Letters* he physically confronts what disquieted him in contemporary civilization, the dominance of technology. Technique has created an alternative universe, self-sufficient and almost independent of *given* nature. Only recently, with our spectacular achievements reaching an unanticipated apex, have we come to understand Heidegger's assertion that technology, more than being our supreme accomplishment, has become a destiny that subjugates its human creators as much as their creations. Guardini forefelt this when in *The End of the Modern World* he described us as "withering beneath the destructive hands of modernity." In the *Letters* he actually saw the process. At that beautiful lake, Italy's first welcome to the wary traveler who has just crossed the Alps, the classical world begins. Virgil knew it, and for Guardini, born in Verona, it meant a return to the ancient, ancestral land. Yet, precisely in this traditional area of Manzoni's *Promessi Sposi*, economically lagging behind the fully industrialized northern countries, the home-bound pilgrim saw the ravage of a primitive industrialization occurring before his very eyes.

The Como landscape has preserved enough of the ancient harmony that united nature with its human cultivator to remind him of the original meaning of "culture." The old fishing boats still had to obey the laws of water and wind while being harnessed to serve human needs. The ancient earth-colored houses with their light balconies and large fireplaces remained attentive to the wiles of sun and fire. But everywhere, from the noise of motors on and around the lake to its pockmarked shores, a technical alternative, indifferent to nature and unrefined in execution, had begun its invasion. Guardini regrets the loss of the ancient harmony while watching the fateful drift of a self-concsious culture. But he does not abandon hope: out of the demise of the old may emerge a new, more sober-minded attitude.

Gradually his report turns into a meditation on finitude. What can we learn once we have thoroughly conquered our environment? How do we define ourselves now that a different cosmos has come into our purview, a cosmos of which we no longer form an integral part? Paradoxically, the boundlessness of our conquest has made us realize how limited the world that we now call ours has become. A new sense of proportion begins to dawn upon the presumptuous conqueror and, with it, an invitation to allow reality to reveal its own inner meaning. Perhaps a more lasting victory awaits the mind in the acceptance of its place in the whole. If so, it will require a less instrumental, more contemplative approach to nature.

Only in the final pages does the name of God, subject of all Guardini's meditations, appear. The delay seems quite appropriate, for we must recover a sense of the sacred before the sacred name can be heard again. Ultimately the *Letters* aim at regaining an attitude of *respect* for the given inwardness of things — the first condition of genuine religion. They ask to be read in that spirit.

Louis Dupré
Yale University

LETTERS FROM LAKE COMO

The Question

Dear Friend,

Do you think of the afternoon on the edge of the forest where the buzzards had their nest? They glided off into the blue distance. The eye focused on their circlings. The inner life was concentrated upon the eye and carried aloft by the force of the clear and soaring power; our whole being had a vision of the fullness of space. In the far distance the mountain ranges rose up in clear outline, and behind them the land that I had not seen for twenty years was waiting. I realized that if I now went back there as a man it would mean a great deal for me.

We spoke about so many things; our own lives and what had taken place on a general and universal scale merged into one another. I also made an attempt to lay hold of a question that I was running into on every hand. For a long time I had been aware of it, of the way it was gaining force, and I saw that upon our finding an answer to it, a vital answer of being and not just of thought, much would depend for our lives.

When I came to Italy the question had become very severe. All its beauty filled me with sorrow. I am now there for the second time, and I must now try to put it all together. There is so much to this question. It seeks the meaning of what is taking place before us. Its answer confronts us with a decision, and I do not know which will be the stronger, what takes place with its ineluctable thrust or insight and triumphant creativity.

We have considered so many things together over the long years. And thus you know what is behind these many words. That will help me. Nothing can be definitive. It is as if I were in the middle of a wave. It is everywhere breaking and rolling and sinking and rising again. I want to see if I can find direction and a path. I want to know what is happening in the thousand forms and events of our day. I feel that I have a part in it so profound that I was terrified when this first became clear to me. I must know what is at issue. You know the saying of Oedipus when he was questioned by the Sphinx and his life depended on finding the answer. It is as if we were being questioned in that way, I, too, in person. I do not know where the question will lead. I will begin and go forward step by step.

I had hardly reached Italy before I felt that I was being addressed by something very significant, including an element that made me very sad. What Europe *is* was before me; what membership of a people is — blood, no doubt, but also loyalty and spirit; what humanity and the world are. Often it was as if these things were real ground on which I moved, real air, real space, as necessary to life as the space outside and the air I was breathing are for the body. All this was great and strong, not the sad part. The sad part was that I felt as though a great process of dying had set in around me.

How can I put this to you? Look, what has already taken place up in the North I saw beginning here. I saw machines invading the land that had previously been the home of culture. I saw death overtaking a life of infinite beauty, and I felt that this was not just an external loss that we could accept and remain who we were. Instead, a life, a life of supreme value that can arise only in the world that we have long since lost, was beginning to perish here, as well as in the North.

As I walked through the valleys of Brianza, from Milan to Lake Como, luxuriant, cultivated with zealous industry, encircled by austere mountains, broad and powerful, I could not believe my eyes. Everywhere it was an inhabited land, valleys and slopes dotted with hamlets and small towns. All nature had been given a new shape by us humans. What culture means in its narrowest sense struck me with full force. The lines of the roofs merged from different directions. They went through the small town set on the hillside or followed the windings of a valley. Integrated in many ways, they finally reached a climax in the belfry with its deep-toned bell. All these things were caught up and encircled by the well-constructed mountain masses. Culture, very lofty and yet self-evident, very naturally — I have no other word.

Nature, then, has been reshaped, subjected to mind and spirit, yet it is perfectly simple. As I have seen again and again, this is how culture as this reshaping affects the conduct of a very simple person in both word and behavior, though he or she may have no particular self-awareness of this. It is part of such a person's blood and development, the legacy of a thousand-year-old process in which culture has developed naturally. I do not know where to find the words to express this miracle that is so full of light and that is as self-evident to us when we live in it as the air and the sun. It is an atmosphere in which everything is set, a rhythm soars over everything, a mode of being exists in which humanity thrives. *Urbanitas:* this word means strictly "city living," a city atmosphere, yet one in which a nobly shaped humanity can flourish. Here nature can pass over smoothly into culture. There is nothing alien or *antithetical* to culture that must wither away if this humanity, this *urbanitas,* this art of living is to come into being. I cannot find a way to express how human this nature is and how we feel in it the possibility of being human in a totally clear but inexhaustibly profound sense.

Yet all at once, then, on the singing lines of a small town, I saw the great box of a factory. Look how in a landscape in which all the risings and fallings and measures and proportions came together in one clear melody, along with the lofty bell tower there was suddenly a smokestack, and everything fell apart. You must take some pains to understand this. It was truly terrible. We are used to it in the North. We have even learned to see something valuable in what is unavoidable. Our eyes are beginning to open to the greatness of this new world, and we are finding the ability to contemplate it and the hands to mold it. But see, here it was totally different. Here was form closer to humanity. Here was nature indwelt by humanity. And now I saw it breaking apart. I thus became aware of what I had not been in the North because previously I had become accustomed to such things. The world of natural humanity, of nature in which humanity dwells, was perishing. I cannot tell you how sad this made me. It was as though we had found something we knew as a precious life and now we were seeing it go under. Here I began to understand *Hölderlin*.

I have a plain sense that a world is developing in which human beings in this specific sense can no longer live — a world that is in some way nonhuman. And I fear that those here in the South will never be able to master it. I am afraid they do not have the grim seriousness, violent power, and inner alertness to the monstrous that is demanded here. The world of machines comes from the North, which also provides its motive force. In the South it will bring naked barbarism.

A time that is sinking is always sad, but sorrow is

especially profound for a life which is doomed to perish and which we feel belongs to us. With it the possibilities of living go under, too.

Inexpressible beauty is here, but it gives me no joy. I do not see how any understanding person could find joy in it.

Artificiality of Existence

Dear Friend,

The first impression remains. It becomes deeper. People rejoice at progress. Of course, it brings them work and food. Many who would otherwise have to emigrate can stay at home. Much need and many impairments in institutions disappear. Automobiles cross the seas, factories grow in numbers, electrification goes forward, all things are fabricated. I told someone what this meant for those from the North; there was understanding. But the destruction that accompanied this progress was seen as necessary. Indeed, bitterness entered in: "Our country has to remain poor and our people emigrate so that you may fulfill your romantic needs here." I had to admit this.

Nevertheless, what is taking place is dreadful. Am I boring you? You know that when someone has a very personal question on the heart and it is suddenly set out in objective historical form, it is impossible to dismiss it. The problem of culture is such to me, and it is becoming increasingly clear to me here. Look, we have never had any relation to nature in an untouched form. Carl Schmitt in his brilliant book on romantic Catholicism (I read it on the journey here) has rightly seen that the longing for untouched nature is itself a product of culture originating in the over-artificiality of existence. In truth, nature begins to relate to us only when we begin to indwell it, when culture begins in it. Culture then develops and, bit by bit, nature is refashioned. We create our own world, shaped by thoughts and controlled not merely by natural urges but by ends that we set to serve ourselves as intellectual and spiritual beings, an environment that is related to us and brought into being by us.

Still, what is the present relation of this human world to the natural world? It is necessarily one of increasing distance. The human world is putting natural things and relations in a different sphere, that of what is thought, willed, posited, and created, and always in some way remote from nature — the sphere of the cultural. We live in this cultural world. In nature "untouched," in the order in which animals live, we have no place. To be human is to have mind and spirit at work. But the human mind or spirit can create only when it has in some way taken over from nature its onward pressing reality, if I might put it thus. The human mind or spirit can create only when the sphere of natural reality has to some extent been released by that of the consciousness, of the ideal, only when it has been challenged

10

and rarefied by this. I might object that the mind or spirit is still reality and must still be able to lay hold of the unweakened reality of nature. Nevertheless, all intellectual and spiritual activity presupposes a kind of asceticism, of breaking up of nature, of dissolving and dematerializing it. Only then can we do our human work.

Thus culture seems from the outset to have about it something alien to nature, something unreal and artificial. This element becomes stronger until it runs up against a limit, the supreme measure of a spirit-filled culture. This culture is remote from nature, as is essential in such a relation, and yet it is so close to it, tied to it so elastically, that it remains natural, and natural juices may flow within it.

I will try to give examples so that what I say may not be too abstract. Take a vessel sailing on Lake Como. Though it is of considerable weight, the masses of wood and linen, along with the force of the wind, combine so perfectly that it has become light. When it sails before the wind, my heart laughs to see how something of this sort has become so light and bright of itself by reason of its perfect form. I do not know what historians make of it, but it seems credible to me when I am told that boats of this kind sailed already in the age of the Romans. We have here an ancient legacy of form. Do you not see what a remarkable fact of culture is present when human beings become masters of wind and wave by fashioning wood and fitting it together and spanning linen sails? In my very blood I have a sense of creation here, of a primal work of human creativity. It is full of mind and spirit, this perfectly fashioned movement in which we master the force of nature. Certainly, we pay for it already with a certain remoteness. We are no longer plunged into the sphere of wind and water as birds and fishes are. The Dionysiac surrender has been reshaped. I have read somewhere that among the fisherfolk of the South Seas there are those who on broad boards dash into the breakers for the enjoyment of it. What an infinite intoxication of kinship with nature must come over such people, as though they were water creatures or part of the waves! In contrast, in the finished sailing vessel, a certain distance from nature has already occurred. We have both withdrawn from nature and mastered it. Our relation to it is now cooler and more alien. Only in this way can any work of culture, of mind and spirit, be done. Yet do you not see how natural the work remains? The lines and proportions of the ship are still in profound harmony with the pressure of the wind and waves and the vital human measure. Those who control this ship are still very closely related to the wind and waves. They are breast to breast with their force. Eye and hand and whole body brace against them. We have here real culture — elevation above nature, yet decisive nearness to it. We are still in a vital way body, but we are shot through with mind and spirit. We master nature by the power of mind and spirit, but we ourselves remain natural.

Nevertheless, let the remoteness from nature become greater! It grieves me when I see built into one of these vessels, these noble creations, a gasoline engine, so that with upright mast but no sails the vessel clatters through the waves like a ghost of itself. Go even further and the sailing vessel becomes a steamer, a great ocean liner — culture indeed, a brilliant technological achievement! And yet a colossus of this type presses on through the sea regardless of wind and waves. It is so large that nature no longer has power over it; we can no longer see nature on it. People on board eat and drink and sleep and dance. They live as if in houses and on city streets. Mark you, something decisive has been lost here. Not only has there been step-by-step development, improvement, and increase in size; a fluid line has been crossed that we cannot fix precisely but can only detect when we have long since passed over it — a line on the far side of which living closeness to nature has been lost. While that original example of human culture which we called a boat or a ship was a work of the mind and spirit, it was also fully integrated into nature.

That type of culture, constantly fashioned afresh by the vital action and movement of the whole person, is no longer with us. In the sailing ship we had a natural existence, for all the presence of mind and spirit in the situation. We had our being in a natural culture. In the modern steamer, however, we are in an artificial situation; measured by the vital elastic human limits, nature has been decisively eliminated. Once there was an order, a living space, which made possible a human existence in a specific sense. On the steamer that is no longer present. We can no longer be seafarers in the first and special sense in which seafaring is a basic form of human existence filled with its own content. The crew members of a liner are not essentially different from employees on the assembly line of a factory.

Do you understand this? Let us take another example. In older Italian houses, especially in rural areas, you will always find the open hearth. We have here something that is bound up with the deepest roots of human existence: seizing open fire and putting the flame to use to warm us. Mind and spirit are at work here; nature is put to human use, and an element of human existence is achieved. There is a payment in some remoteness from nature, to be sure. I am aware of the roar of fire and the primitive power of uncontrolled flames. Here we have a softening and thinning out and distancing. That is the cost of culture. But nature is still close at hand. We still have here a flaming fire that people have kindled and keep burning. We note the situation of the hearth, the enclosing and protecting chimney walls, the living air current, the hearth's organic integration with the room and the house. This is human living. With some exaggeration we might say that being human means lighting a fire at a protected spot so that it may give light and heat. We are in the sphere of primitive humanity here — Prometheus! But note how we have left all that with our coal stoves that we light in autumn and keep burning in clocklike fashion until spring, or with our steam heating, which completely anonymously keeps the house at a certain temperature by means of a boiler. Or think of heating by electricity, in which nothing burns at all, but a current comes into the house and gives warmth in some way. The manifestation of culture has gone, the link with nature has been cut, a totally artificial situation has been created. Everything that was achieved by human existence before an open fire is a thing of the past.

Think of the plow. It, too, is a primitive cultural artifact. How did this implement with the animal in front and the farmer behind turn up the soil? In a purely secondary way, I as a city dweller have seen the mystery of humanity as plowmen worked across the field and tore up the earth to make it receptive to the seed. Profound culture, yet very close to nature. Creative mind and spirit closely interwoven with nature, and in this way the purest humanity. But what happens when the hand plow is mechanized? Certainly this is a wonderful work of technology, and it gives us more bread and raises the standard of living. But riding on the tractor is different from following the plow.

I might offer many more examples. Think of the light given by an open flame. A little while ago I was in Munich. We were in the dining room of an old chapter house. It was lit only with candles hanging in a circle from the ceiling or held in the hand or set in candlesticks as needed. I was able with this light to see in a living manner the beauty of the baroque room. And in it we were in an environment that both enclosed us and received what we had to impart. It then became clear to me that with our gas and electric lighting what is finest in ancient buildings no longer comes to life. How everything became alive in the living light, in a light that constantly battles darkness, that holds warm color and movement in the flickering flame. In such a light the room constantly comes to life afresh. It has foreground and background. The force of the light is graded from brightness close to the flame to the remaining darkness in the heights and corners. And when we move through the room all the strata and levels are set in motion in such a way that we note how little a building is something finished, how much it is something always in process of becoming.

In all manual work we find the primal phenomenon of culture that is human but close to nature. Now compare the smithy with our factories and their electric machines. And compare carpentry and bricklaying with concrete or prefabricated housing. Compare the work of the cabinet-maker or wheelwright with the division of labor at a Ford factory, which breaks down the products into small parts that are produced in vast numbers daily.

In the former we have culture, a work of mind and spirit, yet still close to nature. In it we are creative and stand breast to breast with the things and forces of nature. Here we are human in the deepest sense of the term. But this human culture has almost disappeared. We no longer have wheeled vehicles pulled by animals, with all the vitality that is in them and around them, but automobiles. Moreover, to a large extent doctors are no longer in living touch with the nature at work in the body, using its resources to heal and strengthen — think of the wonderful doctor in Stifter's *Aus der Mappe meines Grossvaters* or the old *Schnarrwerk* in Raabe's *Lar!* Medical thinking and action today so often move only in the pharmaceutical and mechanical sphere of formulas, preparations, and prescriptions. Our foods have largely been made artificial. We have now broken free from the living order of times: morning and evening, day and night, weekday and Sunday, changes of the moon and seasons. We live in an order of time that is our own making, fixed by clocks, work, and pastimes.

The sphere in which we live is becoming more and more artificial, less and less human, more and more — I cannot help saying it — barbarian. The profound sadness of this whole process lies over Italy.

Abstraction

Dear Friend,

I will pursue my train of thought. Today, however, you will need a little patience. I cannot proceed without a little private philosophizing, and usually that is not very good in a letter. I should not be boring for long.

Here in this world I am everywhere personally addressed. From the world of the German Middle Ages to the influx of technology, it would be natural to say the same. Physical images are present. I live among them and have a vital relation with them. Chattels, houses, streets, and cities are like personalities. Family habits, customs, festivals — they are all there with their own forms.

I compare this with what has now developed, the language of newspapers and books, the architecture of cities, the names of streets, houses and household furniture, even human beings, in the whole way in which they gather together on festive and joyous and serious occasions, in the way in which they dress and move and greet one another.

And I see that which is physically shaped and distinctive disappear. Everything is becoming impersonal. A strange unreality is coming over human beings and things.

As I look at all these matters more closely, I note, of course, that they are already at the root of all cultural creativity. In my last letter I spoke of the way in which all culture is bought at the cost of immediate vitality. Pursuing this thought, I now say that all culture is bought at the cost of vital reality.

What I have called remoteness from immediate vitality means also that we take a piece of nature, either within us or around us, and with it we move out of the sphere of the most immediate reality into another sphere. In this new sphere things are no longer directly detected, seen, grasped, formed, or enjoyed; rather, they are mediated by signs and substitutes. All culture involves our moving from transitory individual cases to that which endures, from what is unique and nonrecurrent (alongside other such things) to what is infinite, comprehensive, and universal. This process is a matter of not having to wrestle with some definite and unique situation or danger or possibility of action and then with a second and a third and so on. Rather, we want to move away from the particulars that occupy us to what is structured, so that we may adopt an attitude that is right in many and, if possible, all cases, and in this way master the whole of the reality around us. In this process we move away from direct encounter with things, from direct grasping and being grasped, and arrive outside a connection between the ego and things. We no longer lay hold of individual things directly and become stuck in them. Instead, we replace concrete and individual apprehension with comprehensive summary. We thus remain in the sphere of substitutions, signs, and aids, in an order that is no longer the one originally and directly given, but that is now secondary and derived, artificial and abstractly unreal.

Yet a thought strikes me. Is this path to the universal intellectually necessary? By penetrating to what is individual, cannot the human spirit achieve what it seeks, the essential? Are the unique and transitory, on the one hand, and the universal and enduring, on the other, equal but antithetical modes of reality? They are not. There are two ways to the essential, that of the unique and transitory and that of the universal and enduring. And we cannot follow one way apart from the other. We find the essential in the unique only when we are also open to the manner in which it is present in the universal. But we see our way clearly only when we detect the essential also in specific, transitory, and nonrecurrent individual features. Hence, a proper investigation of the unique in our search for the essential is not in advance the same as merely being immersed in what is there. Culture develops when we press on from what is simply there to what is meaningful and essential. Yet that can take place only by means of an act that covers both poles, the particular and the universal, even if the case of specific situations and people may predominate and result in a specific form.

Now I see my way more clearly, and I may take up my theme again. How does the transition take place from the purely factual to the essential, wherein we seek a general understanding and context for that which is enduring and universal? How can this occur without abandoning the relation to the specific, but in such a way as to enable us to see and grasp the multiplicity? We see individual things as instances, get behind them, relate them to other individual things, and posit a representative sign for them that points to what is similar in them. This sign is a form. I add that it is only a form, an abstract form, not a living form such as we have in the leaf of a plant, in an animal, or in the performing of an intellectual act. The latter forms are full of life; they are modes of unique and concrete reality. But the representative sign is a mere form, a concept, a mathematical formula, a device. It does not fit any individual case fully. It presents only certain features, as many as are needed to show what is meant, still leaving our gaze and our hands free for other things that are similar but not the same. It is possible in this way to achieve a comprehensive survey and evaluation of all these things and hence to lay hold of them and master them.

The cost of this mastery, however, is vitality. We are now no longer in the first living relation to corporeal things and people; the relation has been attenuated. We are in an abstract and artificial world, a substitute world, an improper world of significant signs. These signs no longer relate to

22

this specific thing but to all things of this type. Universal signs, then, abstractions. We now live only in the abstract. And is it not true that the abstract is not mind and spirit? Mind and spirit are life, universal, no doubt, but in a living way and therefore comprehensive in a living way. They see what is alive in its uniqueness, yet also as a revelation of that which is everywhere at work — the individual as a self-enclosed unity, yet one that is integrated into the total context. Mind and spirit are not abstractly universal like a formula that fits all things of the same type. They are life; they are concrete. Concepts, however, are abstract, mere forms, signs, abbreviations of thought, means of simplification, and, in a final sense, aids. Our minds and spirits need concepts because we cannot simultaneously grasp the totality of individual things and address each of them in its concrete vitality, because we cannot accept the universal as the total and comprehensive, because we cannot see the specific simultaneously in its uniqueness and in its abiding essence and necessary meaning. It is God who does not need concepts; he sees.

What the concept is for knowledge of things, mechanisms, instruments, and machines are for practical action. What concepts do for knowledge — i.e., grasp many things, not in their vitality, but only by means of posited signs that rightly indicate common features — machines do for action. Machines are steel concepts. They lay hold of many things in such a way as to disregard their individual features and

23

to treat them as though they were all the same. Mechanical processes have the same character as conceptual thinking. Both control things by taking them out of a special living relation to what is individual and creating an artificial order into which they all, more or less, fit.

In other words, all culture has from the very first this abstract aspect. Yet when modern thinking in mathematical concepts arrived and modern technology came into the world of action, this aspect became predominant. It became normative in our relation to the world, our conduct, and therefore our being.

Here in Italy I have seen the dividing point between the ages. I did so when I saw, along with the sailing vessel, a motorboat on the lake, floating, streamlined, but still a machine. I saw this dividing point also when in Padua I went through the streets with their houses that were so full of vitality. In almost all of them the second story rested on pillars and the first floor was set back. The spaces were conjoined, so that on both sides of the streets we had covered walkways. Each house was built individually and yet in such a way as to create a feeling that they all belonged together. But then in the midst of them I came across a modern house of poured concrete, nonorganic, schematic, abstract, and, for all its practicality, barbaric. . . .

Consciousness

Dear Friend,

I detect it again and again: the air is lighter here. It really is. We take life more lightly, too, than you do up north. It is as if life moved more directly from its center into time, into work, into cheerfulness, into sickness and death. It is fuller life if you take the word *life* in its simple and pregnant sense. Up north we are so often troubled about life; we think about it and work out systems by which to live it properly. Many books are then written, many lectures attended, many methods are evolved and followed, until desperately little resembling real life is left. But how long will things remain as they are here in the South?

I will try to get closer to the core of the question at issue. What I said above has this implication. It has become clear to me here that life has become conscious for us. Consciousness is part of culture. It is perhaps its first presupposition, the plane on which it develops. All the things I spoke about earlier are possible on this basis. Culture presupposes distance from direct reality. The decisive act, however, by which we distance ourselves from this reality is that we become conscious of it. Everything else follows. We adopt a position, we set a goal, we find means. Only on the basis of consciousness can we freely lay hold of the world creatively to shape it.

Yet here again is a fine boundary line. In the Middle Ages and the centuries that followed, quite apart from strict learning, there was a profound and subtle knowledge of the self. Sharp scrutiny of the self was made, clear things were said, deep relationships were opened up. Nevertheless, if I compare the attitude of that culture with our own, the intellectual attitude that I still find alive here in Italy along with the average attitude in Germany, a monstrous type of consciousness presents itself to me.

You need to realize for once how extensive it is. I will simply mention familiar things, but note clearly what they mean when taken together. Think of the study of history. One piece after another of our past is evoked. With increasingly sharp methods traces of past ages are found. With ever more refined tools connections are seen and one phenomenon is linked to another. There is increasing ability to detect the bearing of processes and words and gestures, the revelatory significance of customs and artistic and technical relics. We are becoming increasingly aware of our human past in all the fullness of its details and relationships. With more and more knowledge we integrate ourselves into this nexus, ourselves in our age and our age in the total sequence of ages.

We are also becoming more and more conscious of the place where we are. Country after country has been explored. Asia with its historical context has become familiar to us. The North Pole, only a short time ago a mythical point, has been reached. The Gaurisankar has been scaled. Where for Indians the inaccessible height of the throne of the gods once stood, engineers and officers are doing geographical work. The astronomical context of the earth has been established. I am not speaking now of science in the specific sense but of what may be found today in the average consciousness. Earlier the earth was the world, and around it was the mysterious vault of heaven with the hinterland and unknown depths and heights. In the consciousness of many people today, however, the earth has its astronomically exact character as a heavenly body.

Moreover, we are beginning to see the distinctiveness of peoples. We are beginning to relate the European peoples to Europe as a whole and to see the relation of Europe to greater units. We seem to see developing of itself a global consciousness in its first outlines.

Or think of statistics. This is simply a method of achieving awareness. Take in hand the large volumes of national statistics. Bit by bit they offer a record of the nation, its way of life, its qualities, its needs, its possessions, its relation to the world around. We are made clearly conscious of all these things. Numerous cross sections and longitudinal sections run through the volumes in every direction and bring to light the inner nature of the people as a whole. Researches in sociology, popular psychology, national economics, and government expose the inner relationships and trace back one phenomenon to another.

And we ourselves! With what exactness physiological, anatomical, and morphological investigations track the life of the body down to its hidden foundations. As a parallel, think of the body's coming to consciousness from another angle, as in, for example, rhythmic culture. And on the basis of both, remember the search for a vital medical science. On the one hand it involves analytical knowledge deriving from scientific integration, on the other hand a consciousness of the living whole that uses images and senses things. Yet both join as individual members and movements in the total structure from which they derive.

Then there is psychology. We think of the new research into the bordering territories of bodily and intellectual happenings, the sharp discussions aimed at grasping the puzzling level on which these happenings interact. We think also of psychoanalysis, which has discovered beneath the sphere of the soul — which has claimed almost exclusive attention thus far — a further sphere of which only masters of the life of the soul, artists and others, have been aware. There is something abrasive about this. Psychoanalysis is like a newcomer. It has not achieved the ethos that is set for it, its true responsibility, which its great accuracy does not supply. What a high-minded, respectful, and cautious human attitude it does in truth demand! At all events, however, it has brought to light a new sphere of the living soul and has indicated its profound relationships. And how the soul has achieved greater awareness thereby! Take also the discipline of religious psychology. Here wide fields have come into the light of public consciousness that previously were purely inward. Facts and relations are now open that once were hidden.

I want to emphasize once again how all this concerns me here. I am not focusing on true learning in such matters, or on the specialized work of scholars, but on the fact that consciousness, awareness, has now become and is increasingly becoming the universal attitude. The developed system of education — and among us education still means acquiring knowledge — beginning with school in every form and at every level, then going on to lectures, books, journals, guidance, and travel, is a systematic process of developing awareness. Science passes over into the consciousness of the people.

Newspapers are a technique of developing awareness. By them we today become aware of what is going on around us and to us and in us. Reporters are present at events to describe and integrate them. Cameras take pictures of them. Nothing happens anymore without being noticed. The decisive point is that we accept all this as normal. Moreover, our literature — especially short stories and novels — as a process of developing awareness in artistic form, often becomes pure scientific analysis. And note the popular substitute — it has been this so far — the film. There you will quickly see a distinctive psychologizing, a desire to bring out, relate, and emphasize psychological processes.

Everywhere, then, we find an attitude in which we not only are and live and act but also know all these things, know the reasons for them, find the relations, and see the inner mechanisms of what takes place. This attitude is indeed basic in every sphere, from the setting of technological goals to immediate living, to recreation and amusements. Consciousness is our attitude, our atmosphere. And it is becoming increasingly so.

In the last decades a trend has set in that seems to contradict this. In philosophical, psychological, and pedagogical thinking, and even in problems of natural science, an antirationalistic movement has asserted itself. This movement refuses to reduce everything to concepts and formulas. It stresses, rather, the suprarational nature of the quality, the characteristic form, of the organic, of the soul, of the personality. The suprarational is stretched to the point of the irrational, of what is antithetical to concepts. Is this, then, a return to nonawareness? Only in appearance. In truth the development of awareness is making a decisive advance here. For it is again a development of the consciousness that these sides of being are seen so clearly, that there is a realization that here we cannot achieve anything with the methods of the concept. To see so clearly how special scientific approaches must relate to the special nature of such objects, to demand such special approaches and techniques, and to do so with a feeling for their reach, bearing, and position within the total life of learning — though this might seem to be regression in the development of awareness, it is in reality a decisive breakthrough to a new consciousness.

What does all of this mean? I recall going down a staircase, and suddenly, when my foot was leaving one step and preparing to set itself down on another, I became aware of what I was doing. I then noted what self-evident certainty is displayed in the play of muscles. I felt that a question was thus raised concerning motion. This was a triviality, and yet it tells us what the issue is here. Life needs the protection of nonawareness. We are told this already by the universal psychological law that we cannot perform an intellectual act and at the same time be aware of it. We can only look back on it when it is completed. If we try to achieve awareness of it when we are doing it, we can do so only by always interrupting it and thus hovering between the action and knowledge of it. Obviously the action will suffer greatly as a result. It seems to me that this typifies the life of the mind and spirit as a whole. Our action is constantly interrupted by reflection on it. Thus all our life bears the distinctive character of what is interrupted, broken. It does not have the great line that is sure of itself, the confident movement deriving from the self.

Still, let us probe deeper. Plants can grow only when their roots are in the dark. They emerge from the dark into the light. That is the direction of life. The plant and its direction die when the root is exposed to the light. All life must be grounded in what is not conscious and from that root emerge into the brightness of consciousness. Yet I see consciousness becoming more and more deeply the root of our life. A relation to other lives is seen, one event is brought under the same law as others, and we get closer and closer in our scrutiny to the beginnings, the origins of life. The root of life itself, what is innermost to it, is lit up.

Can life sustain this? Can it become consciousness and at the same time remain alive?

Survey

Dear Friend,

I note that my letters are changing. At first I could illustrate from the many forms around me. Now I am enmeshed in the problem. Concepts thus come on the scene, and these are abstract. But this is how it must be until we achieve the masterly simplicity that speaks on the basis of vision and pure vitality.

In the last letter I spoke about the consciousness of our age. It was not just a matter of many people today knowing many things. What seemed important above all to me was that consciousness is becoming an attitude, a basic feature, of our cultural life.

This fact has now come home to me from another angle. We survey ourselves and the world in which we stand. Something new and decisive compared with the past has entered our total political situation, namely, the fact that we can survey the earth. It has become a closed field of political events and actions. Naturally the earth has always been known as one of definite extent and limits. But only now — World War I contributed largely to this — has a sufficiently large number of people become aware of this. We now note that we are in a space that cannot be extended.

Perhaps there was already at an earlier time some first stage of such an awareness. What later antiquity called the *oikumene*, the total space of the inhabited earth, seems to point in this direction. The idea of a total inhabited or inhabitable area was present, and political intentions and cultural creativity oriented themselves toward it. This notion went well with the global impact of Greek culture, and the thrust of this activity, rather than its actual size, lay behind the global political character of the Roman Empire, similarly the global character of the British Empire. Yet something decisive was missing in the notion. It did not, in fact, have the whole earth in view. The *oikumene* was encircled by the uninhabited areas of the earth, and a sense of this played a part in the whole idea. Possibilities of extension were still present, unexploited areas, undiscovered resources. Things are different today. The *oikumene* is now definitively present. We realize that the area in which we live and work can no longer be extended. We have the whole earth in view. There are no more possibilities of expansion, no more reserves.

Wholly new political problems result if we take the word *political* in a sense that thus far, I believe, only the Romans and British have understood. What is now demanded, however, goes far beyond what was called "politics" even in the Roman or British sense. It seems to me that it has only now become plain what politics means in its most exacting sense. Our outward human existence is now beginning to come under frontier pressure because we can no longer expand into anything around us, because the boundaries have become absolute. Questions of relations are now urgent in the total sense, and these are the true political questions.

For example, how do the forces at work in a limited field interrelate? Where do we find the essential order and integration? The fact that the earth confronts us as a definitively limited field of a specific size gives rise to a distinctive pressure from *outside*, a frontier pressure, whether national, economic, cultural, or indeed intellectual and spiritual. This pressure gives distinctive importance to all intrinsic points of integration and forms of relationship. And it especially gives political importance to, for example, humanity, the cultural circle, the nation, and personality, indeed, to the congregation and the family — for I do not believe that anything in these is outdated. On the contrary, we have in them even more essential principles of order. Totally new problems are posed. New attitudes and arts are demanded if we are to solve them. Only those people can be real politicians who know how the forces and forms of order at work relate to one another, who have them in view and can work with them.

We have also become aware of the different peoples

and cultural spheres. A distinctive cultural-political attitude is forming that sees the uniqueness of peoples and cultural spheres and asks how they relate to one another. Questions like the following are becoming more and more common: What happens when Indians with their own distinctive intellect and spiritual life enter into a working partnership with the West? Earlier, Europe saw in its own culture an absolute and self-evident standard by which to criticize other cultures. But it is now ready to accept criticism from Asia and America because it sees that this is justified. The day of naive Europeanism is over. In all areas, artistic, social, and religious, we detect a strange uncertainty. The unthinking complacency of Europeans has been shattered. And the self-awareness of Orientals has been awakened. The attitudes and achievements of individual peoples are set in the critical light of the totality. All these are signs that the idea of a closed field is forming on which the different peoples with their cultures can stand and work together.

Or take a people or state as a unit. Survey is again a distinctive fact. A highly developed statistical technique used by a system of government that is divided into departments has achieved a grasp of the total situation as regards economic goods, achievements in labor, social strata, national resources, educational processes, and intellectual and cultural forces. What distinguished World War I from all previous wars was precisely the thoroughness with which all available resources were seen and employed. Note the network of the provisions of Versailles! Increasingly the problems of the economic, cultural, and social leadership of one people become those of the *oikumene.* Questions about what resources, realities, and orders are present, how they relate to one another, how the whole is made up of the parts, and how again it is at work in every detail are extending to the common field of the *oikumene.* Politicians have to be able to survey a larger and larger field. The view of the whole must become increasingly clear. They must have an increasingly clear feeling for details and an increasingly sure feeling for the art of bringing everything into a possible relationship that is also essentially the right one.

Our relation to history is taking on the same basic character. Consider the approach of historians to it, even those who might only teach it. Once again, you will soon come across survey as the distinctive fact. Gaps, of course, open up everywhere. But we know where the gaps are. They are part of the total picture. We have become decisively aware of history as a total unit. We see it in profile as an infinitely complicated web of various creative forces and processes. We see it lengthwise as a total line with branches that we detect with increasing clarity. How secure we are beginning to feel in regard to the totality of history is shown by the more and more refined and numerous historical connections we make. The great sections are made up at every point of thousands of interrelated threads. It is as if we need less and less the aid to orientation that sharp differentiations offer. Where we have the totality, what we previously had to differentiate for the sake of orientation may now slip back into the total flow, and even without such differentiations it may have a sure place in the stream of a history that flows on in smooth transitions. Historical problems seem now to have left behind the age of discovery. I have in mind the age of important findings, when new sources and monuments were constantly opening up new areas and creating new points of contact. Instead, we now have the age of comparison. Increasingly the questions are those of more penetrating analysis, linkage, and structure.

In relation to nature, too, the period of discovery seems to be passing, the digging into unexplored fields ceasing. Discoveries, at least, do not have the same dynamic role in the total attitude as they did twenty years ago. I am no specialist, but I sense in many areas of natural science a feeling that the most decisive things, laws, forces, and forms are already there to see. New ages of discovery might come later, but now, it seems, is a time to take stock. For example, geography has, in a very tangible sense, an essential knowledge of what is there. Moreover, zoology and botany for the most part no longer count on finding hosts of new plant and animal forms.

We note a very puzzling fact. It seems to be one of those facts that show us most incisively the unsystematic, incomplete, purely factual, and one might almost say capricious character of our existence. I refer to the fact that these and only these substances are present, these and only these forms, shapes, qualities, and laws. We can give no reason why it should be these and not others, or why there should be so many and not more or less, or why they should be as they are and not otherwise. This is the deep riddle of the reality that is there, that is as it is, that is not necessarily but inescapably real. (In history this truth has at times an almost unbearable edge to it!) We see that these things and qualities and orders are there — they and not others, so many and not more. We have to accept this. Chemistry and physics dig ever more deeply into depths and details. But there is not the same leaping as before from one area to another as one new force or law after another is discovered. The question that seems to be at issue more and more is that of inner relations. The total picture has to be sought and presented. It is as if the human mind could approach the sphere of reality accessible to it and not measure it — for to claim a measurability would be to negate the incommensurable nexus — but find in it a kind of frontier. It is as if the human mind had in some way achieved a sense of all that is immediately possible for it.

Strictly one ought not to write such things. All specialists can make it clear to us how culpable it is to play the dilettante. But I will let what I have written stand by way of clarifying what I now want to say. All of it might be decisively significant for our whole being and creativity. Perhaps what I called the *oikumene* in the political sphere, a time for provisionally taking stock in the historical and scientific spheres, a movement away from the extensive to the intensive — perhaps such things are only parts of something much more comprehensive, of a new cosmic consciousness that is developing. The older view of a "world," of a closed and beautifully formed and ordered cosmos, perished when the human mind and spirit looked into the reality that reaches off into infinity. The idea of a graspable global unity had to go. A new global feeling is now arising, but of course on a different level. We again descry cosmos, not as a conceptual theory, but as something direct and vital; not as the sense of an enclosed reality that we can comprehend. We know that on every hand we are enmeshed in something that goes further. But to me it is as if we had a sense of some sphere of existence that is allotted to us, a sphere of humanity, of which we have taken possession. This is again a cosmos, but in a new sense we see it as being without astronomical limits. It is a cosmos seen from a human perspective as the living room that we have been assigned as a field related to our own specific powers of knowledge and creation.

We have kinship with ourselves. We know ourselves to some extent. We can survey in our consciousness the way we are made up anatomically, physiologically, and psychologically. Certainly new breakthroughs are still being made today. A purely mechanical view of the world is being left behind. Nonmechanical elements are emerging at all points.

We see nonderivable quality along with mere quantity. We see that which cannot be integrated into like units. We are aware of living spiritual, creative, personal features that we cannot trace back to what is dead or what simply exists or what is merely a matter of emotion or impulse. All such things are finding a place in our picture of the world, which was previously one of mechanisms and masses. The mechanical components are not forced out, but we are given the task of seeing and considering how the mechanical and nonmechanical orders work in and with one another.

This is a task of surveying and shaping, one bigger than the mechanistic view of the world ever suspected. We see this task also in our awareness of one another. Old ideas pushed out by mechanistic views of the body and soul are again coming to the fore and calling for integration. This is true in medicine, psychology, pedagogics, and sociology. Still, none of it is new. An older insight that was crowded out has won a place for itself again. What all of this amounts to with regard to both the world and ourselves is finding out how forces relate to one another — quantity and quality, counting and creating, machines and life, things and persons — whether in detail or in their totality.

This naturally demands that we take a new attitude, a new sense of relations, of measure and limits, of change, of presuppositions and implications, a wholly new feeling for gradation and rank, for compass and context. I am convinced that just as our political methods will appear clumsy to a time not far distant, so this same time, perhaps, will not understand how we can be so stolid in questions pertaining to the investigation of body and soul, or, more correctly, of human beings, as was the case in the nineteenth century and is still to a large extent in the twentieth. A wholly new power is needed to see aspects of reality together, to relate to the world in soul as well, in a way that was simply not done yesterday and is not being done today. Perhaps we need to give a wholly new dynamic to the word *human* — you recall what I said in the second letter.

I return to my theme. It seems to me that the work of extension that was our first task has been done. In it we have at least reached a point where we have the feeling that we must now take a new tack. We must switch our work to the intensive. We must move on from the multiple to the nexus, from extension and survey to depth.

Mastery

Dear Friend,

I have come to realize so clearly these days that there are two ways of knowing. The one sinks into a thing and its context. The aim is to penetrate, to move within, to live with. The other, however, unpacks, tears apart, arranges in compartments, takes over and rules. Still, the matter is not as simple as that. Even the first way of knowing involves possessing, enabling those who know to get a strong grip on things. I spent the whole afternoon walking on the peninsula that separates the arm of Lake Como from Lake Lecco. The events in Manzoni's *Betrothed* took place here. Many of the names are thus well-known ones. How human beings have taken over this stretch of land! The tracks follow the hills, hurry across them, press close to them, and course their own plastic movement. The gardens climb up and down the hills, nestle in their folds, spread out over them. The shrubs and trees, often selected, obey the directions of soil and light and present a finely formed and scented picture. Every curve of land, every view of the lake is used, and somewhere at the heart of this sphere of life is the villa, and in it are people with open eyes and hearts.

These are not moneyed folk who regard an automobile as more important than a noble piece of human existence. Rather, with lively attention they get a feeling for all this growth and development and swelling and blooming. How nature has been possessed and seen and understood here! How it obeys the hand that unconsciously knows it! How the trees grow up in most noble shapes without artificial means! How the landscape follows the will that forms it and commands that more and more of it become a dwelling place, a more vitally flourishing and responsive space for human life! The mastery is gentle. It is irresistibly strong, for it courses through the filled nerves of nature, but it is gentle. Its manner, I might almost say, is like that of the soul as it builds up and controls materials and powers for the body.

The other form of knowledge and its mastery is very different. It began to emerge already during the Renaissance but has really come into its own very recently. This knowledge does not inspect; it analyzes. It does not construct a picture of the world, but a formula. Its desire is to achieve power so as to bring force to bear on things, a law that can be formulated rationally. Here we have the basis and character of its dominion: compulsion, arbitrary compulsion devoid of all respect.

The first way of ruling began with investigation, then noted connections, unleashed forces, realized possibilities, emphasized what it desired, and, stressing this, repressed other things. It was a knowing, validating, stimulating, directing, and underlining of natural forces and relations. All that it gave form to was still in some way nature. Mind and spirit were certainly involved; human purposes, views of reality, and essential relations were put to use. But all of this was always in organic connection with nature. It was rule by service, creation out of natural possibilities, which did not fail to transgress set limits or observe final directions. But now, in accordance with the formula discovered, energies and masses are put to use in the proportions desired. They are detached from their organic links and arbitrarily pressed into service. The new desire for mastery does not in any sense follow natural courses or observe natural proportions. Indeed, it treats these with complete indifference. The new mastery posits its aims arbitrarily on rational grounds — or are there still links in the aims that it posits, links not yet observable? Does another way of being natural exist that we are not yet aware of? Do different proportions and character occur that are thus disruptive of what has obtained thus far? But enough of that! Today at least what we seem to have is caprice. No inner relations are manifested. And since a formulation of natural forces is at work, obedience can be arbitrarily enforced.

By their nature the new knowledge and creativity are a

knowing of possibilities and a mastery and compulsion according to capriciously set goals. Modern physics and chemistry have established this kind of mastery over materials and forces. The latter must obey. What holds sway is not a vital and sympathetic power, an ability to follow the inner courses of reality and to shape it accordingly. Instead, mechanistic laws are present that have been established once and for all and that anyone may manipulate. Materials and forces are harnessed, unleashed, burst open, altered, and directed at will. There is no feeling for what is organically possible or tolerable in any living sense. No sense of natural proportions determines the approach. A rationally constructed and arbitrarily set goal reigns supreme. On the basis of a known formula, materials and forces are put into the required condition: machines. Machines are an iron formula that directs the material to the desired end.

Time and space are made subject as well as materials and forces. They are mastered by means of communications. What is to come is calculated in advance, and what has taken place is preserved.

In addition, the new biology — the doctrine of the conditions and determinative influences of growth, of genetic laws and the laws of development — has become a technique and is taught both theoretically and practically. We thus achieve a working rational mastery over plant and animal life. With regard to the nobility of achievement, what came earlier was probably superior. But this new way is more universally teachable and can be technically clarified and reduced to fixed methods.

All of this — and I stress this point — is not a special inclination of individuals but the general attitude of our age. It is the acknowledged goal that we find in fixed approaches, in measures and efforts that are irrefutable and have become our natural bent, hardened into structures of cultural life that are all-determinative.

We see the same phenomenon in politics. Here statistics provides the basis. A host of bureaucrats makes use of statistics and governs by this means. Newspapers, put in the service of goal-directed slogans, mold public opinion; so do posters and films. Similarly, the monstrous organization of economic life works rationally and arbitrarily like a machine. It both serves politics and controls it. It has a profound impact on cultural life by means of the radio, the control of the press, theater, music, and travel, etc.

A powerful network of educational plans and prescribed courses and methods gives direction and character to instruction and education, and on the basis of state control forces everything into the system. This system, by increasingly refined psychological and biological researches and methods, more and more inescapably establishes the living substance and influences the moral character.

Thus a technique of controlling living people is developing. Compared to older forms of life this technique is primitive. But it is constructed rationally and embodied in a monstrous system, and it takes charge more brutally than the older forms could ever have approved of. For most of us the possibility of a free development and central shaping of the person has disappeared. A reference to the methods of suggestion might indicate how far this control of living people now goes and might still go.

Much more might be said. We find the same thing in every sphere of human existence and creativity. By rational research modern science finds the laws and formulas for what takes place and applies them in the form of technology, machines, and methods. During the process we lose all the inner contact that we might have derived from a sense of proportion and the following of natural forms. We become inwardly devoid of form, proportion, and direction. We arbitrarily fix our goals and force the mastered powers of nature to bring them to fulfillment.

The older culture, then, can only wither away. What is coming is not just greater and stronger extension, but something different in its whole order and basic attitude. Everywhere we see true culture vanishing, and our first reaction tells us that what is replacing it is barbaric. Only further reflection and a more profound reaction indicate the possibility of a new order in what is now chaotic in its effects, an order of different proportions and with a different basic attitude. But is that really so, or is necessity giving rise to such a theory? Is our shattered sensibility seeking some justification?

At all events, the anxious question arises: What will become of life if it is delivered up to the power of this dominion? Living events go their own ways, ways of development, sensitive, deep-rooted ways. They have their own profound sureness. They are infinitely tender but also inconceivably strong and invincibly powerful so long as they remain in their own essential courses.

But these courses are now heading for the dark. The creativity is now unconscious. Things seem to be following no rule, to be taking place simply at will.

What will happen when these events become subject to the harsh consciousness of rational formulas, the power of technical compulsion? A system of machines is engulfing life. It defends itself. It seeks free air and a secure basis. Can life retain its living character in this system?

The Masses

Dear Friend,

We have sailed in a rowboat from the middle of the lake to the end of the arm. We were on the lake over eight hours following the shore with its localities and gardens and villas. What riches! There at Bellagio was the Villa Melzi with its wonderfully beautiful garden. Not much further along the Viale Giulio made its broad ascent to the villa with ancient cypresses on both sides. In this gloomy corner of the lake, very silent, is the Villa Pliniana, going back, I think, to the sixteenth century. Its loggia drops steeply to the water. Its mighty cypresses and the villa itself are full of the endless murmur of a spring, for this spring, once described by Pliny, is the true mistress of the house. Finely set in the lake and fully lit up by the sun is the Ponta del Balbianello. And so forth. Noble works based on a noble humanity and making human life that can find no breath elsewhere possible.

We spoke about these works with a joy tinged by bitterness and a feeling of being shut out. My brother said to me: "All that is now gone. It can be there only so long as there are a few to enjoy it. Art is only for the few. Once the masses come, it perishes." I tried to refute this, and I now see even more clearly what is wrong with it. But is there not oppressively much that is right in it? True culture — but is all culture true? Certainly that earlier culture was true culture, whether political, artistic, social, philosophical, or religious, and it was undoubtedly owed to a few. What speaks to us so strongly from the past was the work of a small aristocracy.

It seems to us that the past was the source of a great flood of work and achievement. In truth, the plenitude was that of significance, power, and attainment, an intensive plenitude. This past work is, in fact, not very great numerically when we take into account the time taken to produce it. We find only a small number of paintings, buildings, and writings, of political, social, and religious institutions, compared to the mass of what we find today. I might simply recall that Berlin alone has as many buildings as all Greece. Athens, for us a picture of unheard of greatness, was only an average city in size. How many books were written in the whole history of Greece and Rome? How many literary works have the Middle Ages left us? Indeed, how many endure even from the classical age of more modern literature? The number was small compared to the many works that are published in Germany alone in a single year.

Thus only a few works but a concentration of force

from within the people was possible. Now I do not think that a people numbering two million has double the creative power of a people of one million. It may have in terms of mechanical addition, but not in terms of living creativity. Numerical growth does not proportionately increase creative depth. Less numerous peoples in antiquity and the Middle Ages had more concentrated creative force than larger peoples today.

While individuals have their own energies, so do total groups. But has a people, or the whole race, unlimited creative energy? Or is this energy thinned out by the number of individuals? Are individual and group energies related in some way? Does it make no difference to the creative power of an individual whether there are many individuals? It is very doubtful whether we can apply standards of measurement to life and spirit. What this means we can feel rather than clearly state. The total cultural work of our own time represents a massive achievement by one measure. But in the tiny sphere of, for example, Greek culture, the truly creative element has depth and force of a very different kind. And because less was created there could be a purer concentration of force. There was greater fullness and more thorough outworking. The forms and the problems handed down from generation to generation came to completion.

Creation also proceeded more slowly. Recall how in *Dichtung und Wahrheit* Goethe's father built his house only after long consideration, reflection, and preparation. The

53

case might be unusual, but it did not essentially transgress the general norm. How long a cathedral took to build! How slowly a city came into being! And looking at the larger picture, how slowly history takes its course, the stream of living development, the transmutation of governing types, the forging of relations and forms in thought and life. Almost imperceptibly a style emerges, reaches a peak, and ebbs. This is how typical artistic forms ripened, the problems of thought, the modes of social order. The possibilities they contained could be realized without either force or haste. Growth could take place as with a tree that knows the time it needs and in the course of the year produces leaves, blossoms, and fruit, and with the seasons adds to the trunk and branches, thus taking shape as a whole. Working forces could fully assert themselves, the powers of a people, the influences of landscape, the living tasks that are set at a given time in history.

The various things integral to life found their appropriate forms. Palaces became palaces as dwellings of inner greatness; houses became houses, churches real churches. The living forms of a feast day in both attitude and appearance could develop and distinguish it clearly from an ordinary day. Government could really be government with its own form. The same may be said of discipleship and obedience. The special contents of individual spheres of life had a time in which to emerge clearly and find their right expression.

Rankings formed. Individual vocations had their own value and dignity, but that did not prevent recognition of higher and lower vocations. Similarly, final equality before God did not prevent the formation of classes on a scale of intellectual ranking. Life was strongly grasped, and vocational work was done. But that did not involve any confusion of the everyday with the sublime, of the profane with the sacred.

Fixed attitudes and ways of thinking developed. The classes had their own specific tasks and rights and ideas of worth. Schools emerged with traditions that had undergone lengthy development and become a living legacy. There were workshops and guilds with traditional skills, with abilities that had become second nature in ways of working and creating. There were ancient families in whose corporate lives certain specific images of life and work had been formed. These bore historical responsibility. Human types developed, then, of strong and clear content, types of creativity, achievement, rule, service, enjoyment, all disciplined and made capable of playing a full historical role.

Forces were developed in the work of long generations. When we look at the great medieval masters, the tremendous power of constructive thinking did not emerge overnight. Thus Bonaventura in his *Lectures on the Work of Six Days,* delivered to select circles at the University of Paris, first divided one concept into two, then into more and more, until he finally had forty-eight divisions. And he probably lectured extemporaneously and quickly, so that the poor scribe who took the lectures down made mistakes and became confused about his system. Centuries of thinking and listening and speaking and disciplined training were at work to give this power living expression. The architectural abilities of the medieval builders and their workmen did not develop overnight, nor did the powers of religious concentration in the orders, nor the military code of the knights. Centuries were at work here. If a command is to be credible and not to crush the one who hears it, there must be an ability to obey. To be able to live in a palace the blood of rulers is needed. How out of keeping it is if in a noble villa here, with rooms that may not be large but that have the quality of greatness, whose earlier owners were perhaps an elderly couple with many servants, now someone newly rich lives, perhaps from America or the Balkans. The villa and he do not suit one another; he is not at home here. He is like a parasite on someone else's property. But his possession means that the true heirs are shut out. So it is with everything.

Living forms of humanity developed that were embodied in human existence and attitude. These were related to the various works and creations. They emerged and lived in these with understanding and enjoyment. They were responsible for the works and the forms. They saw to it that they had a meaning appropriate to their nature and that they would not be misused, overused, or desecrated.

Finally, all these things had roots. They grew out of the soil, the country, this or that particular country. They grew out of history. With no particular awareness, it could be taken for granted that they would be handed down. Tradition was in time what air and water and soil are in space.

We thus have two things. On the one hand, a developed humanity has slowly achieved clearly evolved forms and has developed powers of seeing, owning, living, thinking, ruling, and creating. On the other hand, we have appropriately formed work, mature and full creation — not a numerical but an intensive fullness. Life pulses through it down to the last member. The multiplicity of life finds expression in a thousand details. Every gate, lattice, and staircase, every proverb, custom, office, and tradition has been vitally formed and produced. So flexible is the creative work! It fits in with the soil and place and historical moment. It divides into different types, classes, human ranks, and seasons of the year. And all of it, material, work, content, is authentic.

But the masses have changed all this. By a truly puzzling process that economic and social commonplaces do not really explain, "human substance" has suddenly exploded in monstrous numerical growth. Perhaps machines are responsible for the population increase of the last six decades. They have certainly made it possible. Yet it is clear at once that we cannot explain the one in terms of the other. It seems to me that the process which creates the machine, bursting apart, as I have said, the organic order, destroying the natural context, and unleashing isolated powers, has also triggered the expansive power of human growth.

Yet what is the result? Many things result and very quickly. Quickly come, quickly go! Especially the latter, for production needs expanding markets. Unregulated production, then, is not governed by the organic interplay of supply and demand. Unlimited production means that every art of force and cunning must be used to produce unlimited consumption! Nothing has time to ripen. Everything must proceed by the shortest and easiest route. Everything is mass produced, nothing individual. Types develop again — no! distortions of types, schemata. Forms are evolved that can be produced most quickly in the mass. I read recently that in a typical American corporation it was laid down that instead of having seventy or eighty styles of a certain article — I think it was casks — they should now make only a dozen. Standardization is the way to go. By his action and writing, Ford has shown this in a way that all can understand. The objects of consumption are slowly being reduced to a few very practical types, whether it be casks, automobiles, houses, clothes, words, schools, or, finally, people. Yes, people too! Look at the world around you. When the Taylor system is perfected, manufacturing will be able to throw unlimited quantities on the market, and everything that has a personal soul, all individually developed creativity, will basically end.

A dreadful confusion of forms has emerged. These forms no longer have roots in life and its essential content. We build theaters in the form of temples, banks in the form of cathedrals, apartment complexes in the form of palaces. Working days and Sundays merge into one another. Work is done in high-heeled shoes and silk stockings. We no longer dress specially for festivals. Employers who try to act as such often make themselves ridiculous because all they have is money. Those of necessarily modest means ape the practices that demand wealth and big houses, but no inner style drives them to do so. Now lofty words are used to say everyday things. Newspaper articles are written in academic and oratorical forms that would demand philosophical investigation if the articles had any content. Solemn addresses bear the stamp of the marketplace. And so it goes on without end. Everywhere we find hybridization. All rankings are lost. We all think we are justified in whatever we do. We are no longer tied to the essence of content or the historical or social dignity of form. Nothing commands respect, and nothing is inviolable. We lay hands on everything. All philosophical problems, all art, all historical events, all personalities, even down to the last hidden thing in recollection, letter, or confession — all are up for grabs. How sickening it is! How vulgar life has become in every sphere, even in religion, for despite the profound equality of the children of God and the fact that all things are theirs, they are unable to prevent the surrender of all *arcana* and the irruption of clamor and bustle into the quietness that alone is essentially creative. How we long for an arcane discipline that will protect what is sacred from the marketplace, including the marketplace within.

And it is not only a matter of disgust! What devastation goes on before us! The *Nibelungen* film may be a brilliant technical achievement, but it is still a horror. Wagner's operas had already corroded the world of German saga. From the days of the Ring, the saga ceased to be an intellectual possession of the German people as it once was, or as it might have become. It has already been plunged down from the lonely heights of the heroic to the sphere of trash, and this film continued the work of destruction. If saga has any meaning it is this: it brings heroic existence before us. But what happens to saga when a modern woman novelist makes a script of its world, and modern movie actors use their own vain and puny figures to represent the saga's heroes? Movie stars are then projected on the screen, and those who see the images have lost the *Nibelungenlied.* That saga has to be recited and heard, and the heroes of it have to be brought to life by something that is heroic in the soul. If we are unable to do this, then the heroes are not there for us.

Here is the aristocracy of a work of art. Such a work does not spring to life for those who are not related to it in some way. But here everything is made showy and trashy — and the more hopelessly so, the greater the technical perfection. So it is with everything. Whatever figures of history or art films lay hold of they destroy. They bring them all into the trashy sphere, that is, within the reach of the masses. I do not understand how anyone can see value here. If the film only did what ordinary popularizations of literary works and historical processes do, then it would simply be a vulgarizing of something valuable. In truth, however, it lies essentially on a different plane. If movie theaters tried to show what a film's true creative task is, they would soon be empty.

Take religious drama, the ordinary mysteries. Just a few more of them, a few more years of legends and religious lyrics, and our life of faith will no longer be healthy. What is the Christmas event when it is reduced to sweet nothings in a hundred nativity plays? How we tear apart all the mysteries of our faith in hymns and legends! Perhaps someone will say that they must be weak then; we should not be able to destroy such things. But I see and hear, and trash is as sticky as flypaper. It clings to the brain, and endless pains are needed to be rid of it. Think only of the frightful religious pictures in churches, on calendars, and in pious books of all kinds. How the figure of Christ is distorted so that decades are needed to break free from the clinging artificiality!

Or think of speech, words! Newspapers, posters, propaganda, and addresses are all at work and cause devastation. Some years ago the word *edel* (noble) was a highly prized one, and it was used sparingly. It was realized that what this word expressed was something rare and isolated and superior. But today in various combinations (*Edelgasen, Edelkommunisten, Edelstahl*) it has been adulterated, and the climax has come with *Edelschnaps.* I feel that something is lost when a word for which there is no replacement is brashly misused on our streets in advertisements for liquor. And then we have other words like *Mensch, Leben, Wert* (man, life, value), and so on — a whole series of destructions! And how we desecrate sacred words such as *revelation, grace, God-man,* and even *God.* How shamelessly they are tossed around and are made to serve the emptiest needs of second-rate writers who want to puff out their little ideas.

To me it is as if a terrible machine were crushing our inheritance between the stones. We are becoming poor, very poor. What is not wholly genuine in itself and in our own soul is going to pieces. And yet it has to be so. Perhaps it is only in this way that we can arrive at what is truly essential.

Devastated things, words, forms, and people! We have rulers, and many of them do not have the right attitude for their job. In many houses people live who are not suited for them; they merely inhabit them as though they were dressed in clothes that belong to others. They enjoy things, but to the sound of hearty kisses. They issue orders, but with inner uncertainty, sharpness, and arrogance. They want to be autonomous, but only in the form of petty revolt. They speak about lofty things, religious and philosophical, but they do so mistakenly in a way that is journalistic. They criticize, but they do not ask with what validity they do so, how long they have been engaged in thought, whether they themselves have known the discipline of creativity. And so it goes on! Only now do we see how ugly and corrosive is all that we were referring to in the earlier letters.

From a literary point of view I am not up to this. I wish I did not feel these things so strongly. Nevertheless, I must continue. Walter Rathenau has written a terrifying book, *Die neue Gesellschaft*. In it he speaks of the new incursion of people from below. The destruction this will cause is incalculable because so many of those who are surging up have so little by way of legacy that what repels us as trash seems glorious and attractive to them. I am not hitting at such people. I feel only guilt relating to them. What I have in view is simply the destruction caused by the masses. I realize that what is emerging might have something different in it. The mass culture of our day might also bear some other name, and something great might emerge from it later. But devastation is the present situation. Can we live in it?

EIGHTH LETTER

Dissolution of the Organic

Dear Friend,

Much depends on this present letter. I hope I can succeed in saying what I want to say. There is a narrow tongue of land between the two arms of Lake Como. On its summit — and fine trees grow on it, so that when we approach by water it seems as if we are looking at an old Koch picture — once stood the castle of Serbelloni, an ancient robbers' nest overlooking the lake. On the actual tongue of land below is the Villa Serbelloni, now a hotel, but still choice and charming. The whole tongue of land evidences lofty culture. I come down upon it from a long and silent walk between the hills of Bellagio and San Giovanni, my soul full of the power and harmony that have gone into the buildings, gardens, walls, and roads here. And all these things have forced upon me the question: What is the essence of this culture, and of all ancient culture?

It seems to me that it is this: that this culture is the creation of living people and that it is finally related to

65

nature. I will see if I can clarify my meaning. It will sum up all that I have said thus far. As I see it, all that these people created, all that they surrounded themselves with, all that they did, all their works and achievements, the whole tempo of what happened — all these things were governed by the nature and law of their living constitution. The body with its parts and organs, the soul with its patent and latent powers — these governed it all. Living people undertook to work and initiate and create and possess, whether individually or corporately as family, community, state, or church. For what I have in mind relates also to social orders, processes, and forms.

People did, of course, use tools and aids in great numbers and with great delicacy. But these were only supports, extending the range of activity of natural human organs, making possible more acute and accurate seeing and hearing, working, understanding, and controlling. The means were always integrated into the interplay of the human unit, and a limit was always set to make possible direct and living execution. I cannot say where the limit was, but I am aware of it. I also do not know whether it was a sense of proportion that prevented people from crossing the boundary, a conscious or unconscious volition, a final feeling for self-limitation, or simply a lack of technical ability. Regardless, the boundary was there. I think I have seen signs here and there that at times people were close to crossing it, as in the case of the Caracalla spa at Rome. It seems to me that here we have something that really belongs to our own time. The final stage of the expansion and organization of the Roman Empire gives me the same sense. Perhaps the Romans as a whole were at the point of crossing the boundary. Perhaps they were very close to the sphere of the mechanical. I have similar feelings when observing St. Peter's. In the last resort it lacks life, perhaps because here the organic measure of the human seems to have been transgressed by people who should have known better. This often happens. Yet in the main the limit has been observed, and the result is that all that the ancient culture produced — and it lasted up to the middle of the last century — is still human. In its proportions and dynamics and relations it is humanly controlled. Very concretely the human soul infuses it, and it is a fit dwelling for this soul. It supports us and enhances us, but always within the compass of a final norm.

This culture is also natural. Now all human creation involves taking something out of its immediate natural context and putting it in an artificial sphere. Nevertheless, ancient creativity of all kinds left things very close to nature. It is as if natural forces could still flow unchecked through them, as if things were only partially taken out of nature, as if in what is most important they were still rooted in nature, as if they were lifted out and then the hand caused them to sink back into the basic nexus.

Hence all the things that were made — works, buildings, furnishings, clothes, along with movements, orders, customs, and usages — could fit easily into nature. Even now they do not disturb nature in any ultimate sense. They do not break it open. They are always natural. Even if there is no mingling, for nature and culture are two different things and have to remain different, the things which culture has made can relate to nature. The two notes can ring out harmoniously together.

I have experienced the truth of this so deeply in these days. Below, in a dark corner of the lake, is the Villa Pliniana, a serious work of Renaissance art. A kind of ravine intersects the hillside and nourishes ancient cypresses. The villa fits into the scene. We arrive by lake, land, climb a covered stairway, and reach a terrace. A narthex then leads into the villa proper. We hear a murmuring. We enter the loggia, which is supported by three beautifully formed pillars. It falls down steeply to the lake. The murmuring becomes ever stronger. We then turn round and see how close to the cliff the house is built. Out of the cliff a spring gushes forth that more than once emerges and then is lost to sight again. It is the true mistress of the house. Those who enter are its guests. Truly a great and worthy *pensiero magnifico*.

And then as a counterpart to the villa and its surroundings, in the full sun as the Italians say, we land in San Giovanni and stand on a terrace where a stonemason has his workshop, and we see a finely built staircase. As we go up it and cross the street that runs along the shore, two simple pillars confront us. Between them we see a little hill to which eight approaches lead. We walk ten paces, then approach fifteen finely profiled steps embedded in the turf on both sides. The whole ascent, with the stairway in the middle, is thirty paces broad. On both sides are cypresses, some of them very old, all dark, rising up into blue sky. At the top is the beginning of a road some thirty paces wide, overgrown with grass, with a narrow path to the left. This road takes us five hundred paces between ascending orchards, with a low stone wall covered by wisteria, until we reach Villa Giulia. The ascent is difficult, but how indescribably magnificent! Greatness, breadth, sky and sun, fruitfulness are all around, and all are illumined by the inner power of the creative. At the end we confront a lattice of extreme simplicity. A large garden opens up in a long oval. Around it is simply a path with magnolia trees on the outer edge, and in the middle the round and shallow basin of a fountain. Nothing else! Only space! The villa is astoundingly simple. If you look around, you see that you have crossed the tongue of land and are on the other side. The villa looks across the second arm of the lake and onto the steep and sunburnt mountains of Lecco. All is arranged so that we can walk through in sunshine and cross the hill in a greatness that has been created.

Do you not see here a union of nature and human work? But perhaps you say that such works are choice and rare. I will thus tell you of others. If you go between the

gardens and onto the hill and between many walls — I have
to recall Manzoni's *Betrothed,* for between these walls, which
constantly twist, every twenty paces there are *bravi* such as
waited for poor Don Abbondio and brought such distur-
bance to his terrible life — if we go this way it strangely
gives us courage. It seems as if everything begins to ring
out softly. Every so often there are stairways, shallow steps
with round stones, making it possible for donkeys with their
burdens to climb the hill. How these paths climb and turn
and glide along the hill between continuous walls. And on
both sides we see mysterious and inaccessible glory, and
surely there is further glory behind the walls, mulberries,
olives, bamboo, mimosa, and whatever else can grow and
produce decorative leaves and blossoms. It has often seemed
to me that the walls and paths are simply music. I have felt
this in all my members even to the very blood. What is this?

Yes, and then I have gone across to the other side of
the lake where there are no villas but real farming, often
not very remunerative, for we are high up here, and soon
we reach the territory where people live only off the products
of sparse pastures and the harvest of chestnut trees. I encircled Regoledo and came through a little village, I do not
know where, for the names hereabouts are often very strange.
My path led through the square, and I halted, astounded
by its beauty. Still, if the village became wealthy and acquired a mayor with a touch of modernity it would undoubtedly be ruined. Ordinary houses have been built in

the usual style — no plaster, undressed stone as quarried locally! But the placing of the houses, the way they fit into the tiny square — that is the unheard of thing. Three open streets lead into the square, and we reach a fourth under a house and through a gate. No dead surfaces! Each wall is different, yet all are in harmonious movement and are surely unique in their construction! You will find the same wherever you go so long as the modern age has not intruded. And from such a village you go out again into the fields and vineyards and sylvan glades and down to the lake to find that all is in relation.

It is as I have said. Human beings created all these things; they are thoroughly human. But they have all been taken out of a natural context and so they are profoundly natural. That is the very thing that is being lost.

The following has happened. A century-long search for knowledge of nature has achieved a certain measure of insight into its laws. But that has made it possible to break into the closed nexus of nature. Individual forces such as steam, electricity, and chemical energy have been taken out of their natural context. We know their rational laws, and on the basis of this knowledge we can unleash their power. Something in us corresponding to this rationally unleashed energy — a specific attitude, craving, approach, a desire for mechanical and rational works — has arisen and placed these forces at our disposal, creating for them the intellectual plane on which we can see and exploit them with increasing fullness. Isolated natural forces, on the basis of the knowledge and unleashing of their regular functioning, can now be backed by a new and specifically mechanical desire. When I say *mechanical* I do not mean that the will has become material. There is in this will a monstrous intellectual element. But this will is not organically oriented. It does not operate in the same way as the creative will of the preceding age, which made use of the natural orders of given natural relationships. This will does not presuppose the organic human sphere of taking up and developing. Rather, its starting point is the isolated, rationally understood power of nature, which works through the machine — which itself is no more than rationality reduced to a tool.

Something new comes into being in this way, a whole world of works, goals, institutions, and orders that are no longer determined by our living constitution but by unleashed natural force, by the rational autonomy of this force which goes its own way and no longer worries about any organic standard. This new force is governed by a human attitude that no longer feels itself tied by living human unity and its organic compass and that regards as petty and narrow the limitation in which the earlier time found supreme fulfillment, wisdom, beauty, a well-rounded fullness of life.

This will, this intellectuality, is now so distorted that it can work itself out only in unlimited possibilities as these are rationally unleashed and controlled, put in mechanical form, and realized by natural forces that are compelled to serve specific ends. What results here is no longer something of human creation, at least in the former sense. No longer is any organically human sense of space, form, or relation at the reins, only rational and mechanical logic. The human measure has disappeared. There is no proportion of any kind, whether in big things or in little, whether in the mass or dynamically. The field of outworking is unlimited on every hand. Now freed from every organic link, the will can set its own goals, and by controlling natural forces rationally it can make the execution of these goals compulsory. Living people fall victim to this ineluctability. They are given up to the caprice of their own goals, which have no organic relation.

What takes place here is not human, at least if we measure the human by the human beings who lived before us. It is not natural if we measure the natural by nature as it once was. And you feel how relentlessly what is happening destroys everything that was created by the older humanity and the former link with nature. You see everywhere how piece after piece is eroded, standard after standard is broken, one creation or order is swallowed up in another. In Germany the process is already so familiar to us that we no longer pay attention to it. Only when from time to time we arrive at an old village or a nonindustrialized area do we see what has perished. Here in Italy we can see the incursion everywhere. It must be even harder in the Far East, in Japan, in the South Seas. In these places undoubtedly things of infinite value have perished in the last decades.

We see the steady overthrow of the old world. The roads that I referred to, the ancient roads, would allow only that speed attainable by the bodies of humans and animals. But when, even as I was writing, a road for automobiles began to replace the fine road from Villa Melzi, that very moment the wonderful interrelation of the human and natural was shattered. The new speed, noise, and smell destroyed it. And once barbarism comes we know very well that it will have the last word, and that one day these roads and places will become cities and streets, and the whole landscape will be reshaped by the road for automobiles. The same thing is happening in the Venice canals. The gondolas glided along noiselessly, moved at a given pace, and were attuned to the building and foundations of the ancient city. Now motorboats are clattering along and making an awful stink. Their shape is elegant, but the basic feeling behind them is very different from that which built the palaces. And their speed is out of proportion with the ancient city. It is deeply symbolic that the waves created by their short and harsh beat are more than the foundations of the houses can stand. Modern technology may perhaps save the city, but in truth the motorboat has destroyed it, and what is left is only a museum piece.

So it is with everything. The tempo of life, the style of work, the form of society, the structure of political and civil events — they are all contrary and alien to the older forms, and if they make a place for themselves in these forms they burst the forms open. The older forms, works, and orders are also alien in our day. Speech, social structure, architecture, chattels, customs — they are among us like a kind of precious heritage from the past, and our care of them is like that with which we handle old things, cautious, and yet with some slight disparagement as for no longer living things.

Our age is different from what has come before. It is not different merely as the Renaissance is compared to the Middle Ages. The difference goes incomparably deeper. It often seems to me that the period from 1830 to 1870 is the watershed. All things before that, however different, belong together. They rest on a similar basic attitude, share the same human standard, are integrated into nature and its proportions. What has come since seems to be governed by a different basic attitude, by the desire to set goals independently of organic connections and on the basis of rationally emerging forces that are mechanically put in the service of this desire and its goals.

The Task

Dear Friend,

I have now not written for some time. I have had three or four letters in mind but have not been satisfied with them. Nevertheless, I am in Germany, and it makes good sense that I should sum up here. Almost two years have gone by since I wrote you the first letter from Lake Como at a time when the question I had been detecting for some time laid hands on me, as it were. I believe that I have now mastered it insofar as we can master questions of vital origin. But perhaps I would put it better if I said that I have adopted a position relative to it. And the answer will not be a formula but living action. Beyond that, of course, it will be an event, and I know that I am committed to this. I have learned what decision means. And I know what is effectively new.

All these are things that I tried to express, and two letters were ready, but when I read them over they sounded so empty that I scrapped them. I was unable to relate to the whole question, to point to the decision that must be made, to let the answer grow out of the core, but also out of the living fullness, so as to give body to it. In a few lines, then, I will try to say what directions I see and in what event I believe.

The urgent question was this: In all that is taking place, is a life supported by human nature and fully human work possible? The old world is perishing — "world" in the broadest sense of the term, the epitome of works and institutions and orders and living attitudes. The middle of the nineteenth century was the historical turning point. (Naturally the roots go back much further.) To that world belonged a certain view of humanity that was common despite all the many and great differences. That world was sustained by human beings and in turn sustained them. *Human beings* created it and gave it life. *They* kept it alive in their hands. It was *their* work, expression, object, and instrument, all at the same time. That was culture, and what we still have in the way of culture today derives from it.

But then came new events of a different type, proportion, and starting point and with a different goal. The forces on which they rested were different, and so was their relation to nature. With these new events, the old order collapsed. And those who supported it, whose blood to some extent we all carry, were homeless. Indeed, they dissolved inwardly, for the older world was through them and they through it. The new events did not just break into the objective order as a matter of objective culture. They also and above all broke into our living humanity. The development of technology is primarily an inner human process. Hence we are homeless in the midst of barbarism. This is true when we look at things from the point of view of the past, for that is to feel our environment collapsing, and ourselves with it. It is also true when we look at things from the standpoint of what is new both without and within, for then all is still chaos.

Insofar, then, as the question consciously or unconsciously derives the idea of what is humanly valuable from the older picture of humanity, the answer must be no. The new events deprive the people of the older culture of any possibility of being. Furthermore, the process may be made gentler, but it cannot be arrested. Still, we must press the thought more deeply. Into the ancient picture of humanity and the world has burst a new and very different type of being and event. This new thing is destructive because it affects those who do not belong to it. More precisely, it is chaotic and destructive because those who do belong to it are not yet on the scene. It is destructive because it is not under human control. It is a surging ahead of unleashed forces that have not yet been mastered, raw material that has not yet been put together, given a living and spiritual form, and related to humanity. Mastering such raw materials and forces — collecting, shaping, and relating them, and thus creating a world, culture — is something that those who are oriented to the old world cannot do. They do not have the norms or concepts or power for the task. On the older plane the battle for living culture has been lost, and we feel the profound helplessness of those who are old. The battle must now be joined on a new plane. Totally technical events and unleashed forces can be mastered only by a new human attitude that is a match for them. We must put mind, spirit, and freedom to work afresh. But we must relate this new effort to the new events, the new manner and style and inner orientation. It must have its living starting point, its fulcrum, where the process itself begins.

Are the processes only variations on a common theme, or is something historically new irrupting in them? If it is — and I am convinced this is so — then we must say yes to it. I know what this yes costs. Those who are already naively saying it, and those who are able to make rapid switches, will see in the deliberations of these letters only a romantic looking back, a tie to what is past. This may give them a feeling of complacency. Yet there is a yes to what is happening historically that is decision because it springs from a knowing heart. Such a yes has weight. Our place is in what is evolving. We must take our place, each at the right point. We must not oppose what is new and try to preserve a beautiful world that is inevitably perishing. Nor should we try to build a new world of the creative imagination that will show none of the damage of what is actually evolving. Rather, we must transform what is coming to be. But we can do this only if we honestly say yes to it and yet with incorruptible hearts remain aware of all that is destructive and nonhuman in it. Our age has been given to us as the soil on which to stand and the task to master.

At bottom we would not wish it otherwise. Our age is not just an external path that we tread; it is ourselves. Our age is our own blood, our own soul. We relate to it as to ourselves. We love it and hate it at one and the same time. As we are, so we relate to it. If we are thoughtless, we relate to it thoughtlessly. If we say yes to it in the form of decision, then it is because we have had to come to a decision vis-à-vis ourselves.

We love the tremendous power of the age and its readiness for responsibility. We love the resoluteness with which it hazards itself and pushes things to extremes. Our soul is touched by something great that might well emerge. We love it, and our soul is touched, even though we see clearly its questionability relative to the value of the past age. We must be able to see very plainly what is at issue if with a fixed heart we are ready to sacrifice the inexpressible nobility of the past.

Nor is it true that what is taking place is not Christian. The minds at work in it may often be non-Christian, but the events as such are not. It is Christianity that has made possible science and technology and all that results from them. Only those who had been influenced by the immediacy of the redeemed soul to God and the dignity of the regenerate, so that they were aware of being different from the world around them, could have broken free from the tie to nature in the way that this has been done in the age of technology. The people of antiquity would have been afraid of hubris here. Only those to whom the relationship with God gave a sense of the unconditional, only those to whom the parable of the treasure hid in the field, the parable of the pearl of great price, and the saying about having to lose one's life showed that there is something for which everything must be given up, were capable of the kind of decision for something ultimate that is dominant in science today and in its search for truth even should this make life impossible, or in technology today in its pressing ahead even should this call all human being into question with its transformation of the world. Only those to whom Christian faith had given profound assurance about eternal life had the confidence that such an undertaking requires. But the forces, of course, have broken free from the hands of living personalities. Or should we say that the latter could not hold them and let them go free? These forces have thus fallen victim to the demonism of number, machine, and the will for domination.

In appropriate activity we now have to penetrate the new thing so as to gain mastery over it. We have to become lords of the unleashed forces and shape them into a new order that relates to humanity. In the last resort only living people and not the tackling of technological problems themselves can do this. There are, of course, technological and scientific tasks, but people have to perform them. A new humanity must emerge of more profound intelligence, new freedom, new inwardness, new form, new ability to give form. It must be of such a kind that it already has new events in all the fibres of its being and in its manner of apprehension. The new science may be monstrous, the economic and political organization gigantic, the technology powerful when measured by the standards of living science, economy, politics, and technology, but they are only raw material. What we need is not less technology but more. Or, more accurately, we need stronger, more considered, more human technology. We need more science, but it must be more intellectual and designed; we need more economic and political energy, but it must be more mature and re-sponsible, able to see the details in the whole contexts to which it belongs. All of that is possible, however, only if living people first make their influence felt in the sphere of objective nature, if they relate this nature to themselves and in this way create a "world" again.

We have to create a world again out of the most monstrous raw materials and forces of all kinds. We orig-inally confronted the task of having to assert ourselves vis-à-vis nature, which then threatened us on all sides be-cause it had not been mastered by us and was thus a chaos for us. "Fill the earth and subdue it"; that chaos — chaos from our standpoint — was shaped into a human world.

To the extent that we did this, taking possession of the world and achieving security over against it and in it, by this creativity we have released new forces that had not yet been released by our own attitude and the form of the world we had created. These forces have increased, and now they have unleashed a new chaos. In the spiral line of history we are now over the point where the first task confronted the race, that of creating a "world." We are again threatened on all sides, this time by a chaos that results from our own creating.

We must first say yes to our age. We cannot solve the problem by retreating or simply seeking to alter or improve. Only a new initiative can bring a solution. It has to be possible to tread the path of developing awareness until we achieve an inner standard, not one imposed by external limitations. It has to be possible at the same time to attain a new inner security independent of what is burning in that awareness, an attitude of respect that supports the knowledge, a new naiveté of consciousness, an ability to believe in the midst of skepticism. It has to be possible also to dispel illusion, to see the limits of existence sharply drawn, and yet to attain to a new infinitude that proceeds from mind and spirit.

Further, it must be possible to tackle the task of mastering nature in a way that is appropriate, but also to find a new sphere of freedom for the soul, to give back true security to life, to achieve an attitude, a disposition, a new order of living, standards of what is excellent and what is despicable, of what is permissible and what is impermissible, of responsibility, of limits, etc., by which we can hold in check the danger of destruction presented by arbitrary natural forces.

We must be willing to see the older aristocracy of small numbers vanish, to accept the fact of everything in mass, to accept the fact that even among the masses each person has rights and life and goods, yet also to bring integration and to arrive at a new ranking of value and humanity.

Finally, it has to be possible to follow the technological path to a meaningful goal, to let technological forces develop with their own dynamic even though in the process the old order perishes, but out of these powers of an adult humanity to create a new order, a new cosmos.

All of this has to be possible, but is it realistic? Within the older human level on which we stand it is not. That is why we see helplessness on every hand. There is much zealous work, but one detects impotence. The unleashed forces have to be mastered on a new level, from a new standpoint, in terms of a new view of things. Systems and ideas will not produce this, only human beings themselves. The emergence of a new, free, strong, and well-formed humanity is needed, one that would be a match for these forces.

Is it not fantasy to hope for anything of this kind? Can

we rationally count on the possibility of such a new humanity emerging? Or are we just comforting ourselves with fine
words?

If we look back at our own European past, in the sphere
of immediate recollection we twice see events that might
be called new in this sense. The first was the coming of the
Christian soul. If we immerse ourselves in the forms and
inner constitution of antiquity, then move on to the New
Testament and the writings of the church fathers and the
developing kingdom of the church, and then immerse ourselves in the cultures that arose in connection therewith, we
find here something that was not present before, that had
not thus far been possible for the race, that created a new
attitude to the world, to self, and to things, a new power
of mastery, a new law, a new spirit.

On a different level, the second event was that of the
Germanic essence entering history, and here again we find
something new and real, no matter how distrustful we are
of racial fantasies. This Germanic inwardness was the basis
of a new way of seeing and grasping the world. What I
have in mind here is not a new religious reality. After Jesus
Christ all new religions are literary fantasies. Nor am I
thinking of an ethnic reality. What is at issue applies to all
peoples — no people is left in reserve to offer its own
solution. What we have here is the emergence of a new and
deep stratum of the human. If we were to say to chemists
that now that we know the elements and forces all the

possibilities of mass and energy are exhausted, they would reply that the most gigantic possibility is still ahead of us. This has now manifested itself, just as tremendous energy is released by the splitting of the atom. We have here a symbol of what I have in mind. In the inner human world an analogous deep force has to emerge that will give a new freedom from the world and a very profound way of seeing and relating to it. Then the event might well take place that was not possible on the older level. We reach here a new level.

I believe that this will come. I cannot prove this, but it seems to me that it is giving intimation of itself. We cannot, of course, bring this to pass by individual decisions or organizations. It is a comprehensive historical event even though it takes place in the individual person. It is an event whose starting point is not accessible to us.

There is something I have not yet said. It has to do with image (*Bild*) and education (*Bildung*). We have the sense that everything around us presents no clear image. From the time of the Enlightenment there has been much talk of education, a sign that it is disappearing. What we find is only a caricature. Education has become just a matter of knowledge, very complete if questionable knowledge, well rounded, but becoming mixed on the margins, so that we no longer have pure knowledge but also things that are a matter of imagination, taste, and judgment. Yet the essence is still knowledge. Our educational institutions are means of passing on knowledge. Educated persons are those who have acquired knowledge of all kinds at these institutions.

Yet all of this has little to do with true education, since true education is rooted in being, not in knowledge. The German word for it (*Bildung*) tells us this. The educated (*gebildet*) person is the one who has been shaped by the inward law of form, whose being and action and thinking and deeds and person and environment conform to an inner image. Such persons thus have unity in great diversity. They have the possibility of always finding themselves again in all that they do and in all that happens to them. But educated persons today, thanks to the Enlightenment, lack any such inner image or form. I have just come out of the New Garden, the not very well-known Potsdam park. In it are three lindens, three as in the fairy tale. What noble creations they are, so free and clearly shaped. But alongside them we see that we ourselves have no true shape. I know that there is a difference between people and trees. I am not finally wanting to make education a matter of nature. Perhaps we are not destined for the unity of the self that a complete education can give — in this regard especially, Christianity did not bring peace but a sword — and perhaps our education will be perfected only in eternity. Nevertheless, so much depends on whether educators have real education in mind or are talking about education when they really mean instruction, which also involves a certain discipline of orderliness and training. We are in truth a profoundly uneducated generation. What is still vital in the educational process has come to us from the past.

Now individuals cannot decide for themselves whether they will be educated in the truest sense or not. None of us can count on this privately, for the image or form that dominates us is basically related to that which also shapes the environment. We cannot be truly educated if we shape ourselves in accordance with what is a real form or image but with this form and with the rhythm of our own being we everywhere come up outside against what is strange and contradictory, whether in social institutions and forms, in the order of dealings with others, in speech, or in the forms of cultural creativity. None of us live only for ourselves; we are also members of the totality, and we live in it.

Twice again in the sphere of more immediate recollection a common image emerged in the West that shaped the totality. The first time was in antiquity, the second in the Middle Ages. In the fourteenth century the medieval world began to crumble. The Renaissance, the baroque, and the styles that followed are not without force, but they are latecomers. Weimar has not altered this in the slightest. The decisive point now lies in individuals. Development and work are oriented to individuals and to what is abstract. And true education has had to be sacrificed in order that individuals may be given the importance which it has been the aim of the modern age to establish.

I believe, however, that a new image is in process of

formation, a different one from that of antiquity or that of the Middle Ages, and especially from that of humanism, classicism, or romanticism. It is coordinated with the new events to which we have referred. Further, it is coordinated with the depth of humanity that we hope is coming to the surface. It is coordinated with the new level on which the battle with the forces that have emerged will be fought. And it will be victorious on that level. The new age will be created out of that depth, out of that image.

We see its precursors. We see them most impressively in architecture. It is everywhere heralding itself, and those who listen for it feel it even though as yet it may be unattainable, uncertain, and confused.

Some of those who have been listening can be found in the youth movement. Critics old and new have sufficiently exposed the questionability of the youth movement. Nevertheless, it is intrinsic to the genuine youth movement to be unsettled to the core by the picture that emerges from the depths of the historical. "Unsettled" — the very term indicates all that is hopeless and tragic in these depths. From its outset the youth movement has opposed the mechanization, rationalization, and individualization of the second half of the nineteenth century. Its very essence is to be found in this opposition. It sought organic life, fellowship, and inner creativity. It turned to nature and thus linked itself to the organic forms of the preindustrial age: songs, dances, modes of intercourse, the plenitude of past culture.

The youth movement's whole approach thus had romantic features. Its backward-looking romanticism found a counterpart in forward-looking utopianism, the faith that a nontechnical world and life could be renewed directly out of nature's essential forces. The romantic aspect symbolized this. But gradually division came, and this was made inevitable by the question of which to choose if a choice had to be made between industry and technology and all that belong to them, on the one side, and the preindustrial, precapitalist order on the other. The true romantics opted for the second, but those who belonged to the authentic youth movement chose technology. Even after the choice was made, however, a common front was still presented against the spirit that has thus far destructively misused the true mission and nature of technology. A fight was waged to give vital meaning to technology.

A true youth movement is not a romantic restoration of the past but a living adumbration of what is coming. It opposes mechanization but feels confronted by the question of whether this mechanical age is not the old age but itself in the full sense part of the new. The movement's demands for simplicity and authenticity came to be misunderstood, however, when they were confused with precapitalist and preindustrial culture. Many a one took this view and led others astray. But the genuine demands for authenticity, simplicity, soberness, brotherliness, etc., are quite compatible with what is being created in modern manufacturing and industry. The demand is that this essential element be taken out of the hands of those who distort it into something nonhuman and misuse it as such and that it be given back its true role. Hence, the deepest desire of the true youth movement is in harmony with the coming age. This is actually confirmed by the fact that this same youth movement is in conflict with what is unspiritual and nonhuman in the new thing in its first phase.

In the light of this attitude and picture it is possible to tread the inwardly foreshadowed cultural path to the very end, the path of knowledge and growing awareness, of surveying, mastering, and technologically transforming nature as it is immediately given. But all of this has to be newly and vitally related to humanity so that a world can be created again that is capable of sustaining humanity. I believe that I can find pledges that this is possible. I see buildings in which technology has been given true form. This form has not been imposed from outside but is of the same origin as the technological image itself, so authentic and self-evident that one might think that a properly constructed machine and a perfectly functional house had already been given artistic form — though this would be a mistaken conclusion since technological correctness is not itself artistic form. This form gives evidence of something greater — namely, that the technological means has been brought into relation to our vital feelings. If we have eyes to see them, there are everywhere advance evidences of the achieving of the great coming form by which the technological will be not merely adorned but truly expressed and molded.

Recently I saw in Wasmuth's monthly journal of architecture a plan for the city of the future that greatly impressed me. The whole form showed technological perspicacity, but it was so austere and powerful that I felt it belonged to us as much as did Memphis, Thebes, Nineveh, and Babylon to their ages. The one who presented the sketch said that in its form the city presupposed the automobile, airplane, and global radio. Extreme technological achievements were no longer disruptive. Rather, they either were a direct presupposition or found a free field.

I see works of art that no longer stand eye to eye with nature as in the modern relation. They do not have the form deriving from the older organic approach. From that standpoint they seem to be very harsh and out of context. But another form is at work in them, and our blood responds to its force. I see individuals who belong to real life today but through whose reason pulsate once again the figures of fairy tales. Think of Friedrich Blunck's stories of the Lower Elbe. Yet we do not have here spectral figures of the night, as in a dream which takes flight from the practical images of modern life. The tales have their origins in machines themselves, and in broad daylight our reality is given that relation to something other which means a fairy story.

I know people who relate with skeptical clarity to

scientific inquiries but who, along with their lack of illusions, still bear in their souls a belief that is not affected by liberal and rationalistic attenuation but derives instead from what is above nature. Newman's greatness was not that he said this or that but that he gave expression to this attitude in his soul. This belief becomes greater and stronger, and under its clear coldness it shelters an inner fire that makes it the equal of the faith of primitive Christianity and the Middle Ages.

In opposition to external drilling and rationalistic teaching I find everywhere a longing for living education. Core points and points of order are forming, and from them a formative force is reaching out. The standards of authenticity, vitality, and essentiality are awakening, and the desire for a new mode of education is present, dubious though the results may yet be in detail. Those who are of this spirit recognize one another for all the differences.

Most hopeful of all, I constantly see individuals meeting one another with a capacity for true brotherliness. No longer the older organically hierarchical form, but also no longer the organization of the last fifty years with its external dividing and integrating! The new types are convincing and self-evident. They are not like the older liberty and equality. There is a disciplined and intrinsic relating. A dynamic core exists that has within it possibilities of order, ranking, higher and lower, yet also of the anchoring of the one in the loyalty and responsibility of the other.

Moreover, I have a sense of increasing profundity. People today are no longer so sure and arrogant in the sphere of physical and psychological reality as they were in the 1890s. It is as if an inner sphere were opening up and drawing us in. A yearning is there for the inward, for quiet, for leaving the mad rush and refocusing. Yet this refocusing will not negate other being and action but will take place within it. We sense possibilities of concentration and inwardness in the everyday, in life as it is. I believe that technology, the economy, and politics need such quiet and inner fervor if they are to do their respective jobs.

Our age is so uncertain, skeptical, seeking, and homeless that there are not a few today, I believe, who stand directly before God. Those who stand in the world have need of a stance in themselves and in something deeper than themselves from which to come to grips with the world again. And indeed a wave is moving out from God and reaching our innermost limit beyond which is the other. It is possible that people may talk together and act and spin out their destinies without a single mention of God, and yet be full of him. In this context the question that faces us will be decided. Will we come to God from the depths of our being, link ourselves to him, and in his freedom and power master chaos in this coming age? Will there be people who place themselves totally at God's disposal and alone with and before him make the true decisions? I detect all of these forces at work. A powerful upsurging, an inner self-opening, an emergence of form on every hand.

Dear friend, what I have written in this letter is weak compared to the question in the others. At bottom I do not know what else to say except that from my heart's core I believe that God is at work. History is going forward in the depths, and we must be ready to play our part, trusting in what God is doing and in the forces that he has made to stir within us.

The Machine and Humanity

I

This address[1] will deal with the way in which, in the process of our cultural development, we are putting the things and energies of nature to use in tools, contrivances, and machines. If that were all, however, there would not be much worth hearing, for in regard to these cultural adjuncts and their construction you know more than I do. My theme, then, will not be so much the actual structure and work of machines as what they mean for human existence, or, more precisely, how their construction and use affect humanity as a living totality.

What I have to say, then, will have the character of an existential problem, and it will thus necessarily reflect concern. We will have to consider primarily the negative element in the phenomenon of machines, the possibility they bring of endangerment and destruction. I ask you, however,

1. The address was delivered in the Munich College of Technology.

97

to see here neither the pessimism that we often sense in current cultural criticism nor the resentment that comes with the end of an epoch against the new thing that is pushing out the old. The concern I want to express is the positive one whether the process of technology worldwide will really achieve the great things that it can and should.

You will surely feel the same concern. A healthy optimism is undoubtedly part of all forceful action, but so, too, is a sense of responsibility for this action. It must be important for you too, then, that we consider the phenomenon of machines in terms of their threatening as well as their beneficial effects.

II

Among the products we are going to discuss we will take the tool first. By a tool I mean something that we relate to the functions of the body in order to enhance what our members and organs can achieve. A rock can deliver a more effective blow than a mere fist. The enhancement is all the greater when the rock is shaped as needed, and even more when it is given a handle, as in a hammer.

From such simple forms, tools of ever greater perfection have developed. Their efficiency has become increasingly strong, exact, and nuanced. An aesthetic element has also been present in the choice of materials and the adding of embellishments, yet expressed also in the way in which the form is adapted to the function. Many tools of this kind have come into being in response to the needs of nourishment, security, and the enrichment of life. Yet essentially the tool was always a functionally related adjunct to the human body, making it possible to do with greater force, refinement, and accuracy what the human senses, members, and organs do.

The next phenomenon in the series is the contrivance. By this we mean an assembly of things outside purely psychosomatic functions that is able to achieve specific goals on the basis of natural forces that work directly. The laws by which this takes place had not yet been examined and understood rationally, but the functional rules were known by experience. For example, teeth can thresh cereals, and so, if two stones are placed on one another and one of them can be revolved, a handmill results. The nature of the device changes and achieves greater strength when the power of water is used in place of the arm, the water being turned over a wheel and thence applied to the millstone in the form of a watermill.

In this way we can isolate functions and objectivize goal-oriented processes in the form of permanent mechanisms. In these the desired work is done without the need for direct human participation as in the case of tools. Around human beings there thus arises a world of contrivances that on the one hand protect human life against the dangers of the surrounding world and on the other hand extend the possibility of direct human action upon nature. By way of illustration one might cite houses, mills, traps, coaches, boats, and so on.

By their nature such contrivances incite *homo faber* constantly to go further. Their working becomes increasingly strong, refined, and exact, their use of materials and energy more economical, their function easier to regulate, etc. From them it is thus an easy transition to the machine.

III

When we have a watermill that works reliably we can say that we have a perfect contrivance, but we can also say that we already have a machine. Strictly, however, a machine is present only when the function is scientifically understood and technically worked out so that the mode of operation can be accurately fixed.

The nature of the machine is more sharply apparent when the energy is not just found in nature — for example, the pressure of water or gravity — but is released from its natural setting on the basis of scientific knowledge and used at will, as with the power of steam, electricity, and nuclear energy.

Machines relieve us of direct work; we need only construct and supervise them. With their help we can take on tasks that are far beyond our own powers and of monstrous size, as the last decades have shown. The special function of one machine comes into relation with that of another, controlling it and continuing it. In this way workshops and factories come into being, and when factories are interrelated we have industry supported by the corresponding sociological structures.

Tools and contrivances rest on processes that are immediately apparent and have functions that can be simply experienced. They use nature as it immediately offers itself. The only problem they present is to find the right materials and adapt them to the required end. This relation to the human organism and to existing nature has resulted in that character of the natural and organic that we perceive as the element of harmony in older cultures. This field of operation of tools and contrivances leads without a break to directly existing nature on the one hand and to directly given humanity on the other.

The more incisively the machine developed, however, the more this reaction was shattered because the processes of scientific knowledge and technical construction came between the machine and ourselves on the one hand and between the machine and nature on the other. These processes have required not only transforming on the basis of experience and manual work, as in the case of the contrivance, but also development by way of scientific theory and complicated technical construction.

With such scientific development, insight into the foundations of nature has become more profound. A lens can magnify small objects and thus enable us to see more. This we can experience directly. But when, on the basis of theory that nonexperts did not understand, microscopes were made, when this theory used the insights of electronics and made things visible that had been known only theoretically before, then between us who use the microscope and the objects that were brought before our eyes was brought a complex process of scientific thought and technical construction. We can no longer experience this directly. Machines are certainly created by people, but the path to them leads by way of such radical changes that the result for the living feelings of those who use them is that the machines seem to be strange and autonomous.

IV

What do machines mean for us then? Without intending any order of ranking we may say first that they offer the possibility of achieving ever higher and more nuanced goals with ever greater certainty. The broad and varied sphere of technological culture has thus arisen on the basis of machines and their functioning. The instruments of this culture make it possible to master increasingly more refined and important tasks of knowledge and labor, and thus to draw nearer and nearer to what one might call the material goal of history, a world that is shaped and controlled.

This steady increase of human power is a directly experienced value. The things of nature simply exist; human beings know it. Things are just there; human beings have life. Natural energy leads to results in accordance with the related laws; yet human beings control the results. As we gain power, we fulfill our humanity. Each successful action brings a feeling of strength, ability, and mastery.

Such human power also means liberation. The ignorant who do not understand nature are prisoners of what is sinister in it. People who do not control nature are subject to the onslaught of its energies. The symptom of this weakness is anxiety, which becomes greater the further we go back into history. As science and technology developed, anxiety waned. We became free; we became the masters.

This leads to the further point that whereas animals belong to the context fixed by their organization within their environment, human beings are basically related to the world as a whole. Naturally, existing historical conditions limit this universality, just as individuals see only so much and can do only what their education and social position allow at any given time. But these limits are relative and can largely be removed, whether by individuals themselves as they strive and learn, by their successors as they improve their situation, or by later epochs as they progress histori- cally. Our human sights are always set on something greater than what is directly before us. Our aim is to master the whole, to lay hold of the world. Indeed, more precise analysis discloses the I-world relation already in limited relations. These are worked out essentially and categorically in such a way that in virtue of our intellectual and spiritual constitution we can break out of the direct context of nature and encounter being, thus grasping objects as a whole and the whole world in the individual.

Machines give visible actualization to this relation to the world. We live today at a historical hour that most impressively brings this fact to light, for by machines we are breaking free from the earth and establishing a relation to space that we could not attain by our own powers.

In the onward course of history, the sociological structures in which we live are extending more and more as clans become tribes, then peoples, then groups and alliances of peoples, and so forth. A feature of the last century was the building of political ideas and impulses on nations, but in the present century the political field has opened up to include the world and to give an awareness of the mutual dependency of all nations. A stage in historical existence is now announcing itself — that of humanity as a whole. The idea of a single human state is still utopian, but the notion of two hostile and warring camps as we now see them perhaps shows us how things might finally go.

This process is very closely related to the fact that the earth is no longer simply the one place of human life but beyond it extends the universe as a whole. The realization that we have this cosmic relation and the realization that we form an earth unit reciprocally condition one another. In the strictest sense, however, it is the machine that has made both possible.

V

Out of what I have said arise serious problems that affect the basis of our existence. In human affairs things never go in only one direction. For each action there is a reaction; every human deed polarizes from the very first. When we do something it is impossible that the effect should remain outside us. We ourselves, in doing it, come under its backlash. Moreover, if I take possession of something and have it, that thing has me, too. We need only recall the psychology of ownership as we learn it from the experience of poverty on the one side and wealth on the other. Further, when I know something, the knowledge affects me. We need only think of the way in which increasing knowledge enhances the courage to live, or the way in which great knowledge that has not yet pressed on to what is ultimate produces skepticism.

Let us now look at some of the directions in which our relation to reality has polarized under the impact of machines. We have seen that machines give us constantly increasing power. But having power means not only that those who have it can decide on different things; it also means that these different things will influence their own position. To gain power is to experience it as it lays claim to our mind, spirit, and disposition. If we have power, we have to use it, and that involves conditions. We have to use it with responsibility, and that involves an ethical problem. If we try to avoid these reactions, we leave the human sphere and fall under the logic of theoretical and practical relations.

Thus dangers of the most diverse kind arise out of the power that machines give. Physically one human group subjugates another in open or concealed conflict. Mentally and spiritually the thinking and feelings of the one influence the other. We need think only of the influence of the media, advertising, and public opinion.

All of this lays upon us a twofold responsibility. Are we up to it? Do we even feel it? If so, then we must give expression to it in the ethos of seizing and exercising power. For this the presupposition is that we freely stand over against machines even as we use them, that we experience and treat them as something for whose operation we have to set the standards. But do we do that? Does any such ethos exist? That remains to be seen. It is a disturbing fact that people often see the attempt to relate to machines in this way as romantic. As a rule today people find in machines and their working given realities that we cannot alter in any way.

Indeed, machines spur us to go into areas where personal restraint would forbid us to intrude. The *Frankfurter Allgemeine Zeitung*, which is certainly not against technology, carried an article that shows us in sharp detail what is the issue here — namely, the possibility of committing people without their even being aware of it. But that involves a basic threat to something that is essential in all human dealings — namely, trust. We read that some time ago industry had told us that it was possible to make microphones so small that they could go on arm bands no bigger than wristwatches. They are now ready for the public and come equipped with faces and fingers. When a salesperson was asked whether people might be bothered by them and would want them, the only counterquestion was: Why should they bother us? Previously only professional spies used such tiny microphones. Today they are produced for everyone. And not a few buy them. We cannot prevent this, but we are permitted to say: "Shame on you, devil" ("Winzige Spione," *FAZ* 9.10.59). The reporter said, "Shame on you, devil," giving evidence of ethical judgment in the matter. But most people seem not to have such judgment. At issue here is not a romantic fear of machines but the fact that power is impinging on something that ought not to be challenged if the very essence of our humanity is to remain unthreatened. The disturbing picture arises of a human life together in which trust can no longer be taken for granted.

A leading article in the same newspaper discussed the

possibilities of private television and made the basic statement that technology can increase dreadfully the element of vice and corruption in the human character. Logic excuses engineers as it has to excuse atomic physicists. But we cannot avoid anxiety lest our designers are now working along lines that will have fateful consequences, taking a direction whose goal is precisely the one that the hidden terror in the human race is seeking. The urge for power and control, the infamous urge to know, and the uncovering of things are going ahead constantly with new instruments and are now coming close to the borders of evil ("Das Fernauge sieht dich," *FAZ* 8.25.59). If they increase, what will such violations mean? The power that ought to liberate us will do the very opposite and rob us of our freedom.

Another question: Will we be able to absorb emotionally our constantly increasing power? The possibility of feeling is not unlimited. We can experience the effect of a shot from a revolver when the one who is struck falls, or that of a grenade when a building collapses, but can we experience that of a dispatched rocket whose flight is simply a mathematically controlled process? Does not this phenomenon belong to a world of effects that is no longer "felt" but merely brought into being?

We speak of objectivity as the most modern of virtues, and by it we mean an attitude that ignores personal feelings and focuses solely on achieving a desired result. And we rightly see here the presupposition on which alone the monstrous tasks that our age has set itself can be performed. But does not this objectivity have a reverse side — namely, the freezing of emotions? That this is true of our situation in general is evident. We might say that all this is romantic, a desire to return to a more inward and restrained form of life, but it might also be taken in a very objective sense, namely, as the question of what will happen to us if we increasingly come into the position of having to suppress our feelings. Feelings will then become weaker, for no living thing remains a living thing if it is put to one side. Again, are the supreme, the truly human values in good hands if they are in the hands of people of that type?

Another phenomenon points in the same direction. Every technical action involves the possessing, using, and shaping of nature. Nature becomes culture. Nature is what is there on its own; culture is what we humans make of it. In the course of history, the culture factor in existence has become stronger, while the natural factor has become weaker.

With the coming of the machine this process has reached a new stage. Nature has been seized and made ready for use. Human beings take a cultural attitude to nature when they go to it. We need only think of photography, which has become the way travelers encounter things, or of the way in which we organize travel and vacations and furnish them with all the amenities of city life.

The process seems to be unavoidable. Still, this question arises: What will be the effect of this constant weakening of the natural factor that still remains in human existence? Each new machine means that something we previously mastered with the help of our organic intellectual equipment is now left to a technical construct. We thus make an object of something that used to be subjective, part of life's initiative. This means release — we are freed. But it means also that we have lost a possibility of creating, of experiencing the world, and of self-development. So long as we had only sailing ships, sea journeys were often dangerous, but they also brought to life the enhancement that goes along with risk. Modern ships have greatly reduced the dangers. They give travelers a few peaceful days in floating hotels. Relative to existence as a whole, is that a gain or a loss?

The fact that the machine brings a measure of freedom hitherto unknown is in the first instance a gain. The value of freedom, however, is not fixed solely by the question "Freedom *from* what?" but decisively by the further question "Freedom *for* what?" Every social pedagogue knows what problems arise regarding use of the time that is made free by machines. If we do not succeed in making meaningful use of the free days, then the result of such "freedom" is negative.

Finally, we need to say something about that which concerns our innermost life. The ongoing intensification of science and technology, with all that this means in economic life, communications, and public consciousness, seems to be a hindrance to our ability to have immediate religious experience or to our receptivity to religious motivation. Some time ago in Westphalia, or so I am told, a motto was in parlance that where the railroad comes, second sight disappears. In an incidental way this seems to point to what I have in mind. Our attention today is claimed for rational and utilitarian tasks in such a way that we can no longer pay attention to that other dimension of our existence.

It is no accident that the worldview which sees in the machine the symbol of fulfilled culture —namely, materialistic communism — is trying systematically to destroy the religious life. It proceeds on the premise that science and technology are the only foundations of existence and that they demand such a level of empirical concentration that everything religious has to be harmful. For positivists who think in terms of Comte's formula for historical progress — lowest stage = religion, second stage = philosophy, third and true stage = science — the disappearance of the religious element is a gain. Those who look deeper realize, however, that this means a loss, not only of an essential part of the human, but of the innermost part.

At the same time, the process causes us to think through the problems of religious existence afresh and to see that the center of a faith approach must be found more profoundly than before in what is truly personal, in the venture and fidelity of decision. But we cannot explore that here.

VI

Out of what we have said very deep and urgent tasks also arise. I can here give no more than an indication of these, but I would like to say that it is most important that you, ladies and gentlemen, who are the present and future leaders in technological initiative, should take note of these tasks.

I am aware that a kind of anxiety exists that leads to distinct distrust of active people. Often this is simply a matter of misunderstanding. Often it comes from those who are still rooted in the era that is passing. And often it is the expression of an emotional romanticism and aestheticism. Still, we should not forget that those who take up practical tasks can indeed very easily ignore the problems. Or else they can have a belief in the power of progress, think that everything will come out right, and feel that they themselves are released from responsibility. In truth, we have here questions that concern our race and its future.

We need to be a little imaginative. Utopias have so often become the reality that imagination is legitimate. Let us imagine an intellectual council of nations in which the very best among us would discuss these matters irrespective of all politics. Human existence has advanced so far, humans have taken so big a grip of themselves, the possibilities of achievement and destruction have become so incalculable that the time has come for a new virtue, a new skill in intellectual government in which, made serious by so much experience, we can break free from entanglement in departmentalized spheres of thinking and life. That is what might take place in these best among us. A living awareness of humanity would make it possible for them to survey human existence as a whole and to consider the *res hominis* with truly sovereign objectivity.

This is utopia, as I said, but utopias are often the forerunners of serious insights and deeds. If I am right, much is moving in this direction. It is disturbing, however, to see how isolated and tentative such things are. In history, creative and unifying forces work more slowly than those that are one-sided and violent, and often that which helps and resolves comes too late. It would be a great favor of history if the clarity of awareness to which education, science, and technology have contributed so much were to prove capable of forestalling all that threatens us.

Bibliographical Note

The letters were first published as *Letters from Italy* in *Schildgenossen* 4, 1924, pp. 333, 335ff., 435ff., and 5, 1925, pp. 17ff., 155ff., 351ff. The address *The Machine and Humanity* was delivered to the Bund der Freunde der technischen Hochschule München in 1959 and first published in the 1959 college *Jahrbuch*, Munich, University Press Wolf and Son, 1960, pp. 59-67.

Printed in the USA
CPSIA information can be obtained
at www.ICGtesting.com
LVHW042345070923
757415LV00003B/538